DRAMA GAMES

Techniques For Self-Development

TIAN DAYTON, Ph.D.

Health Communications, Inc.
Deerfield Beach, Florida
www.hci-online.com

Tian Dayton, Ph.D.
Innerlook, Inc.
New York, NY

© 1990 Tian Dayton
ISBN 1-55874-021-X

Publisher: Health Communications, Inc.
        3201 S.W. 15th Street
        Deerfield Beach, Florida 33442

Cover design by Reta Thomas

Dedication

This book is dedicated to my husband Brandt, our daughter Marina, and our son Alex with deep love and gratitude for sharing their lives and love with me.

Acknowledgments

I would like to say a special thank you to my friend and mentor Sharon Wegscheider-Cruse for all of her love and support, and together with her husband, Joe Cruse, a thank you for their guidance and healing at Onsite.

Thank you also to Rokelle Lerner, Gary Seidler and Peter Vegso for so freely and openly supporting this project and to Marie Stilkind and Elizabeth Wyatt for valuable advice and editing, to Beatrice Manley for being my friend and mentor in the world of drama, Dr. Robert Siroka for support and excellent training in psychodrama, to Dr. Les Halpert and Dr. Lin Goodwin for help and direction with this book, to George Legeros M.B.A. for Greek historical references, Dr. J. L. Moreno, father of psychodrama and action technique and his wife, Zerka Moreno, the doyenne of psychodrama and to my mother, Elaine Walker for introducing me to Al-Anon and the field of addiction at a young age.

Much gratitude to all of the following people for helping me along the way: Marina Dayton, Bill Maloney, M.S.W., Gaile Paige-Bowman, C.S.W., Jo Majors, M.S.W., C.S.W., Lise-Lotte Weil, M.A., Selma Pino-Perry, M.A., Caroline Rob, M.A., Kutzi Priest, Barbara Linder, Leslie Lee, and Jim Murtaugh, Michael O'Brien, Selma Toy and Bill Sowden.

Contents

PART II. GROUP EXERCISES

PART III. GUIDED IMAGERY

Foreword

In working as a therapist and workshop facilitator with both children and adults, I have found experiential games and exercises to be valuable tools. They help group members relax and learn to trust one another or get in touch with their feelings. Games are also a good way to set a mood, break tension or emphasize a didactic point. Sometimes experiential exercises seem to provide a "magic touch" to help a group move in the right direction.

In her guidebook of creative games Tian Dayton reveals some of the "magic" of this technique. She offers clear directions for individual exercises as well as providing important guidelines for using experiential games and exercises. Her format of listing goals, steps and variations for each exercise is an excellent way to allow you to select and adapt games to a particular need.

This book is a valuable tool for therapists, teachers and others interested in learning creative ways to work with groups. The games are adaptable for all ages and would be good for children, adults and families.

Tian has used her background in drama and therapy to create a useful and usable book.

Sharon Wegscheider-Cruse

Preface

Growing up in alcoholic and dysfunctional homes, we learned to numb our feelings. Because what went on around us did not make sense or was painful and confusing, pulling us in all directions, we learned it was better not to feel. Unfortunately when we turn off or numb out painful feelings we turn off good feelings as well. We become very adept at not experiencing our feelings, even pleased at having them under tight control. Within the context of a sick family this was probably a wise survival choice. Later in life, however, we find our "souls are flat."

There is so much happening in our lives that we are only able to participate in half-heartedly. Perhaps we lack the confidence to try something new or, conversely, are unable to do anything twice even if it works for us. We may find it difficult to relax and have fun with our children or friends or to quietly take in the simple pleasures of life. We may be very accomplished outwardly but feel small inside, unable to take pride or derive satisfaction from our accomplishments. Some of us spend our entire lives like this with a feeling of disconnectedness, as if we are watching a movie of ourselves or just going through the motions. Some of us reach out for help, and work toward recovery. We call it recovery because we are recovering what we once had and lost, our feeling selves.

When the numbness begins to melt and feeling returns, the terror is profound. We have kept our finger in the dyke for so long we fear if we remove it the entire thing will collapse. When we numb our feelings, they do not disappear; if they did, their effects would be lost with them. We repress them so they are out of our conscious view. We think they are gone but they are stored in our unconscious and they have tremendous power over us. They can make us nervous, afraid, phobic, depressed, self-destructive, angry or guilty without knowing why. Everything about us *seems* to be fine but we know we don't *feel* fine. In experiential therapy we create situations in which we can locate those repressed feelings and re-experience them. Once we feel them in the present we can come to terms with them and put them in their proper perspective. They become part of our storehouse of understood, accumulated experiences and we derive wisdom from them. It is our experience of life that gives us a sense of participation and well-being. When we are able to center ourselves — enter into the moment with all of our awareness and senses — we know real wealth, inner wealth that we can make a part of our own personal being. The quality of our happiness lies in our ability to experience what lies around us, and in the extent to which we experience our inner selves.

Freud called therapy "the process of making the unconscious conscious." It is this re-experiencing of repressed feelings that gives us back to ourselves. The therapist can set the scene but recovery depends on us and our willingness to choose life.

In her poem "*Renascence*," Edna St. Vincent Millay speaks beautifully to this point:

> The world stands out on either side
> No wider than the heart is wide;
> Above the world is stretched the sky —
> No higher than the soul is high.
> The heart can push the sea and land
> Farther away on either hand;
> The soul can split the sky in two;
> And let the face of God shine through.
> But East and West will pinch the heart
> That can not keep them pushed apart;
> And he whose soul is flat the sky
> Will cave in on him by and by.

Introduction

Since the cultural revolution and growth potential movement of the '60s and '70s, games have increasingly come into use in group settings. They are a natural way of bonding a group and creating trust. They provide an opportunity to experiment with ourselves and others while still in a safe environment.

In our work-oriented culture we leave little time for nongoal-oriented activity such as play and celebration. We have put ourselves in a bind. We have created the most affluent and privileged lifestyle in the world, but we lack the time and ability to relax and enjoy it.

Games not only help us explore ourselves, they are a re-training in spontaneity, deepening our ability to experience and enjoy life.

The Games

There are two types of games in this book. First there are group games that are led by a facilitator and done by the group as a whole.

Second, there are individual pieces either done during group by each group member and then shared with the group, or taken home and then shared with a therapist or brought back to the group.

Use this book as you would a cookbook. Cull from it what you like and vary it wherever you feel like doing so. It should give you the basic information you need and provide a point of departure.

Goals

Experiential games can be very useful in moving a group gently into action. They enable a group to break down initial inhibitions quickly and begin to feel comfortable. A therapist also has a chance to watch how group members behave in the large group games and in the individual pieces that are shared with the group. Thus the games provide a structure for the therapist to get to know group members and the group members to know one another in a non-threatening way.

Role Of The Group Leader

The therapist's job is to create a supportive, safe situation in which self-discovery through experimentation can happen. As J. L. Moreno, the father of psychodrama says, "The stage is enough." The therapist acts as a catalyst between the player and the environment, helping the player help themself by offering the stage as a mirror where the player can experience himself.

Simply speaking out and being heard or seen, without comment or judgment, is part of the work and healing in these games.

The opportunity to experiment with different roles, to "try them on for size," moving in and out of them in a game-like way is important here. The re-education of spontaneity, allowing the "inner child" to become a part of the life of the adult, happens naturally in a playful atmosphere.

The role of the group leader is to be supportive and give each player the feeling that what they present to the group will not be judged harshly. It is also necessary for the leader to create respect for the ground rules and enforce them.

Creating The Atmosphere

The most successful approach to any creative effort lies in drawing on the talent and ideas of the individual. As the leader you will want the environment to be very affirmative. Encourage the players to make mistakes and take risks. We want to create a safe space in which the players will feel free to experiment.

Remember, this manual can be used in either a group setting or with an individual. It can be used:

1. *To sharpen communication skills and enhance self-esteem* — According to current research citing reasons for drug abuse among young people, the most consistent characteristic is low self-esteem. Games help people learn to be in touch with their feelings and give them safe ways to express those feelings, understand and accept them, and build self-esteem. Communication happens on all levels, through body language, voice and attitude. Drama games teach people to communicate more fully and accurately by expanding their repertoire of ideas. It helps them put thought into action through a conscious process that is within their control.

2. *As a stress-reducing activity* — Stress among adults and children is an increasing concern in our society. Adults and children, particularly beginning in pre-adolescence, need activities that help them relax, unwind and enter into that life-giving activity — play. Often our work and school structure systematically removes play from our lives until, as adults, we lose the art entirely and later make awkward attempts to reintroduce it into our lives. Drama games keep play alive.

3. *As therapy for adults* — The play and spontaneity that has been lost in adulthood can be recaptured through drama games. Part of the therapy process is reawakening the "inner child" that has become lost to the adult. We were all children once and we carry that child within us always. If we negate that part of ourselves, we lose our feeling and spontaneity. People who have had great emotional stress or problems often need to validate and recover that part of themselves on their journey to wellness. Drama games offer a safe and structured environment in which to experiment with mood and physical variation.

4. *In the classroom* — Basically this is designed for the classroom teacher who does not have formal drama training. It is used as a new approach to the curriculum being offered and to provide "drama breaks." A "drama break" can provide (a) a change of mood, (b) relaxation and rejuvenation, (c) a safe arena in which to share ideas or feelings, and (d) an introduction to creative work. Probably the most important ingredient in the teaching of drama or its use in the classroom is the attitude of the teacher. Too much freedom can make the work soggy and directionless, too little can make it lifeless and strained. The position of the teacher should be a bit like a spotter in gymnastics. The teacher stands ready to support if necessary. She supervises the situations, provides guidelines and ground rules; but she knows the real impetus will have to come from the children. She can play a very important role in encouraging the children. It also is important that the teacher constantly scan the group, moving in and out of the roles of both quiet guide and active leader. Activities should come one after the other without a break in pattern that will destroy continuity and concentration.

5. *As a "take home" or "learning center" activity* — Some of the material in this manual does not need to be done with a leader. The guided imageries, for example, can be made into a "learn-

ing center" activity. Either the leader or the student can record the "guided imagery" onto a cassette tape: Sound effects or music can be used to make the tape more fun. Then the leader can make the booklet to go with the tape using the examples in the back of the manual. The booklet can include any questions the leader feels are relevant. It is an opportunity for the leader to be creative and to tailor the material to the needs of the group. The book can be photocopied so that each participant will have his or her own. In individual or group therapy the tapes and booklets can be given out by the therapist. I recommend having the cassette and booklets in a flat basket on a shelf along with some colored markers that the players can use for the pictures. The student can remove it from the shelf whenever they desire (along with a cassette recorder) and go off into a private corner to do their own work. They may wish to do this with a friend or in a small group.

6. *As a personal performance piece* — The more comfortable people become thinking on their feet and delivering before others, the more self-esteem they will build. Personal drama pieces give them greater control over what they present and how they present it than in a more structured play and it serves the additional purpose of getting them involved on a deeper level with the material they are presenting. Use the examples for mounting a "Personal Piece"; it will be challenging and stimulating to children and grownups alike.

7. *Games with variations* — The variations at the bottom of each game are one of the most important parts. This is the section that allows the leader to expand in any direction that seems useful or appropriate. The creativity and sensitivity of the leader is always the most important part of any material used. Allow yourself to shine through and have fun with it — the players will be sure to follow you deep into the work.

Ground Rules For The Classroom

Respect for everyone's ideas: This is important in providing a safe space. Children's ideas and feelings are very closely connected and if we laugh at or discount their ideas they will feel laughed at and discounted personally. To create an atmosphere in which they will feel free to open up we need to show them respect even if it means being a little extra patient.

A think tank atmosphere: This means we try to say our idea in just a few sentences and that no one will respond to it as being good or bad; it is simply an idea put out and listened to with no comment or discussion. This will free up the children.

No cross-talk or analyzing another's work: After the initial sharing, cross-talk is any comment made about the shared material. If we get involved with cross-talk we will change the sharing format to a discussion group which is quite a different atmosphere.

Focus on the subject at hand: The subject here is creative work and communication. If the subject veers into other areas gently bring it back. Handle this carefully because an atmosphere that is too authoritarian will be stifling.

No dominating of the group by more aggressive children: Frequently one or two children will not know what to do with themselves in a quiet, centered atmosphere and will act out. Try to keep them in touch with the group; they may need a little extra reassurance that it is all right to do this sort of thing. If you absolutely must you can remove them for a few minutes then welcome them back as soon as possible.

Take a different approach to the subject matter being taught: Teachers, like all of us, get stuck. This will often result in the children getting stuck as well. Children tend to prefer the subjects that teachers love. So use this material to develop new ways of seeing and approaching any subject that you feel it can be applied to.

Close with group sharing: Wherever you feel it is appropriate after group work, finish by asking people to share what they experienced from the work. Sharing is not a time to give advice or criticism. Rather begin by saying "What came up for me . . ." or "How this operates in my life . . ." or share in a letter form saying Dear (the main participant) and at the end of the share sign off giving the name of the sharer. Group members who may have played a role other than themselves may use this time to de-role saying "Hi (name of main participant), I'm not (name of role), I'm (sharer's own name)."

Age Appropriate.

There is a code in the upper right-hand corner of each page indicating what age group each game is appropriate for.

A = Adult or adolescent
C = Children
AC = Adult, adolescent, or children

What Is Co-dependency?

Co-dependency is the pre-personality disorder that develops when someone lives alongside another co-dependent, an addicted person or a dysfunctional person. It is losing of oneself to the pervasive illness. It happens gradually as more and more energy goes into coping rather than growing and living; when defending against painful emotional situations takes precedence over meeting healthy developmental needs.

Co-dependency profoundly affects an individual's ability to have healthy relationships with people as well as with major life situations such as work and play, food, money and sex. Boundaries in the co-dependent tend to be fuzzy and inappropriate. They often do not know where they leave off and the other person or situation begins. Co-dependents frequently have grown up in families where addiction is present but they can be from any type of dysfunctional family. If they are from addicted families they will also be "adult children of addiction." This population courts unmanageability. Indeed, they have been "looking good" and "managing" since childhood, in the absence of appropriate parental management, and this has become their habit pattern. When they grow up they attempt to do the same in their adult relationships. They try to control, fix and direct the people in their lives and then wonder why relationships never work out. They say that they desire peace but have their highest comfort levels with crises and can feel threatened and uncomfortable when life runs smoothly.

Their focus is constantly on taking care of other people and ignoring themselves. Because their needs were not attended to when growing up they tend to treat themselves as they were treated as children, ignoring and discounting their own needs.

This disease has deep, powerful roots that can produce anything from mild dysfunction and inappropriate behavior to violence, incest and highly destructive behavior. Because co-dependents feel they are

1

different, they isolate themselves or hide their pain under a mask of success and normalcy. No one knows how much they hurt inside or how long and how deep they carry emotions of pain, shame and anger. Oftentimes when an addict recovers from their substance abuse they discover it is their co-dependency issues that are the deeper cause of their problems and the next thing to work on.

Growing Up In A Co-dependent Family

The family, to use Virginia Satir's metaphor, is like a mobile. If you make an adjustment to one part the rest of the parts will adjust as well, moving about until it reestablishes balance or equilibrium. If one member of a family becomes ill or changes the rest of the family will change too.

The alcoholic family might be characterized by selective reinforcement. What works one day will not necessarily work another day, rules are constantly changing. Hence family members have a feeling of walking on eggshells, a need to overanticipate or divine the confusing components of a given situation. The atmosphere becomes unreliable and family members feel overwhelmed. They feel that if only they could understand just a little bit better — if only they could make *themselves* just a little bit better — if only they could try just a little bit harder, things would be okay; Dad wouldn't drink, Mom wouldn't cry, brother wouldn't try to achieve so hard, sister wouldn't act out, I wouldn't feel so helpless, alone and essentially impotent. If only. . . .

This chaos and confusion is seldom talked about. Feelings are held inside so long that they become inaccessible even to the person feeling them; they are not expressed and understood. This situation creates a disease called co-dependency. Children who have grown up in alcoholic families carry this disease into adulthood. Statistically, they are four times more at risk for drinking than the average person. But that is not all, their co-dependency illness usually causes them to form unhealthy relationships simply because they feel familiar. Co-dependents can become seriously compulsive about work, food, sex, power, money, children, loved ones, parents and/or mood-altering drugs. For example, they will work for the same reasons that an alcoholic would drink — to relieve anxiety, enhance a low self-image, to numb feelings, create distance, gain acceptance and love and so

3

on. These compulsions will be accompanied by the same type of denial that can surround an alcoholic drinking.

D. W. Winnicott refers to the "good-enough parent." This parent has managed to meet their child's needs satisfactorily enough so that the child could build a healthy personality and become a healthy, productive adult. According to Winnicott, the continued presence of the mother or a mother-figure is essential while the child is accommodating the destructiveness that is part of his or her make-up. "The infant gradually becomes able to tolerate feeling anxious (guilty) about the destructive elements in instinctual experiences because he knows there will be an opportunity for repairing and rebuilding . . . " For the child growing up in an alcoholic family the opportunity for repairing and rebuilding is seriously hampered. Rather than learning how to accommodate inner destructiveness through a stable set of reactions from a mother or father, the parents' reactions are unstable in character. This provokes anxiety in the child and he does not know what to do with his destructiveness. He may find it least complicated to turn his destructive tendencies onto himself or randomly project them onto objects outside of himself. He may begin to develop the same sort of behavior patterns that his parents demonstrate. The tragedy is that both parents will be preoccupied with their own problems and will have little energy left to assist their child in the difficult process of growing up. To further complicate matters, both parties will be steeped in their own denial about their illness and will tend to minimize whatever is going on with their children that might threaten them. One of the only ways the child's pain will be heard is if he seriously acts out. At this point the family will focus on him as the problem and turn him into the scapegoat. This will bring relief to the system and they will again avoid dealing with their sick family unit that has become dependent on problems.

With all this going on it is no wonder that each member of an alcoholic family develops a co-dependent illness with a progression of its own. The good news is that it is being recognized, addressed and treated and that there is a happy and healthy recovery process which not only addresses the illness but is a productive, vital and spiritual approach to a clear and happy life.

He in whom I
enclose my name is
weeping in this
dungeon. I am ever
busy building this
wall all around; and
as this wall goes up
into the sky day by
day I lose sight of
my true being in its
dark shadow.

I take pride in this
great wall, and I
plaster it with dust
and sand lest a least
hole should be left
in this name; and for
all the care I take I
lose sight of my true
being.

— Rabindranath Tagore

I

Individual
Exercises

"Be yourself, that's all there is of you . . ."
Ralph Waldo Emerson

E X E R C I S E 1

Relaxation Exercise

Goals:

1. To allow both mind and body to relax.
2. To create time in the day to be with ourselves.

Steps:

1. Lie comfortably on your back with a narrow pillow under your head, palms facing the ceiling.
2. Breathe in and out easily and completely without a pause between inhalation and exhalation.
3. Mentally go through the following points in your body and ask your mind to ask your body to relax while maintaining breathing: forehead, eyes, cheeks, mouth, tongue, jaw, neck, shoulders, chest, arms, hands, fingers, fingertips, waist, hips, legs, feet, toes and tips of toes.
4. Continue to breathe in and out and allow the relaxation to deepen.

Variations:

This is a good exercise to do before listening to daily affirmations or any tape you choose, or before going to bed or meditating.

E X E R C I S E 2

Journal Writing

Goals:

1. Release feelings in a constructive, safe way.
2. Make unconscious material conscious.
3. Gain insight into oneself.

Steps:

1. Pick up your journal or any paper and pen.
2. Allow whatever you are feeling to surface without thinking about it — just let it come.
3. Put your feelings into words and write them down without trying to sound good or smart or nice — don't edit them in any way.

Variations:

A pen and paper are almost always available to you — at home, on a train, bus or airplane. Wherever you are, short of the shower, you can enter your thoughts and feelings into a journal. This is a very cleansing process and gives us valuable insight into ourselves. Some people may wish to speak their thoughts into a tape recorder.

E X E R C I S E 3

Centering

Goals:

1. Connect body and mind.
2. Become present in the situation.
3. Relax.

Steps:

1. Sit in a chair with your back straight or lie flat on the floor with the palms of your hands facing the ceiling.
2. Focus your attention on the center of your chest.
3. Breathe in and out easily and completely, without pausing between inhalation and exhalation. The inhalation will be shorter than the exhalation.
4. On the exhalation, think of pushing the air out completely and on the inhalation, simply allowing the breath to re-enter the body.

Variations:

While doing this, you can imagine that you are exhaling negativity and tension and inhaling peace and harmony. You also can give the exhalation a color that reminds you of tension and inhale beautiful rainbow colors and light and ease.

This may be done while listening to affirmation tapes, music or lectures.

E X E R C I S E 4

Affirmations

Goals:

1. Replace old negative messages with new positive ones.
2. Create an affirmative state of mind on your own.
3. Create a positive self-image.

Steps:

1. Center yourself and listen to affirmations on a tape.
2. Center yourself and read a daily affirmation from a book.
3. Center yourself and allow an affirmative message to rise from your subconscious. Repeat it to yourself.
4. Write it down and pin it any place that you frequently pass by.
5. Repeat this to yourself throughout the day.

Variations:

Affirmations may seem small but their effect is great. They trickle down into our subconscious and reprogram it for a positive, full and prosperous life. Beautiful work has been done in this area by Rokelle Lerner and Joe Cruse.

E X E R C I S E **5**

Letter Writing

Goals:

1. Work with feelings about another person without involving that person.
2. Work with feelings about oneself in a structured way.

Steps:

1. Decide which type of letter you want to write (see variations).
2. Begin with "Dear So and So" and end with an appropriate closing and sign your name.
3. Write anything that comes to your mind. This letter is not meant to be sent but to fully release your feelings. It works best to simply write anything that comes to mind quickly, not thinking about how it sounds or imagining that anyone will read it.

Variations:

You may write any type of letter you can think of to anyone you want. Here are a few common ones:

1. A letter of forgiveness to oneself.
2. A letter of forgiveness to someone else.
3. A letter expressing anger towards someone.

4. A letter from someone expressing sentiments you wish they had expressed to you.
5. A letter from someone who has hurt you asking for your forgiveness.
6. A letter telling someone how they hurt you.
7. A letter to someone expressing a desire for reconciliation.
8. A letter to someone expressing understanding of what they went through.
9. A letter from someone expressing understanding of what you went through.
10. A letter to your disease self from your recovering self.

This is an endlessly useful exercise. It can help confront feelings that are too threatening even to speak about through the use of writing. One may even wish to dictate if it is too difficult to write it. It is a safe way to relieve anger, express it and let it go. One may wish to share it silently or aloud with a safe person. This can also be used to give a gift to oneself of good things that were never said. This is a tool to move closer to forgiveness and letting go.

EXERCISE 6

Individual Mirroring

Goals:

1. Take a good look at yourself in the mirror.
2. Gain information about yourself by looking.
3. Really see what lies beneath your face.

Steps:

1. Find a mirror to look into where you are comfortable sitting or standing, or use a hand mirror.
2. Center yourself and just look at yourself in the mirror.
3. Observe your eyes, your forehead, the corners of your eyes, the set of your mouth and the way that you hold your head.
4. Notice the mood that your face projects.
5. Be with yourself as a dispassionate observer.

Variations:

Allow the feelings that are evoked by looking at yourself to surface and if you like you may tell yourself what you observe. Later, after you have observed everything in a neutral way, you may talk to yourself and gently comfort yourself. Tell yourself how it was for you and how you would like it to be in the future. Make friends with the image of yourself and become comfortable. Try to like yourself.

E X E R C I S E 7

Inner Child Writing

Goals:

1. Awaken the child within the adult and get acquainted.
2. Release feelings that were repressed during childhood.
3. Rediscover our feeling selves.

Steps:

1. Find pen and paper, a quiet place to write and center yourself.
2. Allow your thoughts to come forward and record them onto the paper as they come, with no attempt to make sense of them.
3. Write in the first person as the child referring to itself, using your childhood nickname and picturing yourself in youth.

Variations:

Inner child work is at the heart of recovery. Anything we can learn about our inner child is invaluable information to our adult selves. The pain we experienced in our childhood can keep us from life but if it is uncovered, re-experienced and understood in the light of today, it will become fertilizer for a richer, fuller life and much wisdom will be gleaned from it.

EXERCISE 8

Personal Inner Child Picture

Goals:

1. Get in touch with the inner child.
2. Gain information about our inner child.
3. Release feelings repressed in childhood in a safe and constructive manner.

Steps:

1. Find several pieces of paper and crayons, markers or any writing instrument.
2. Scribble on a page or two to get comfortable with the materials.
3. Allow an image of yourself as a child to surface and draw it without concern as to whether or not it is good.

Variations:

You may wish to place your child in a setting or include important objects or pets in your picture. You may draw several pictures of your child and things that were important to your child.

E X E R C I S E *9*

Inner Child Poem

Goals:

1. Give a voice to the inner child.
2. Get in touch with repressed material.
3. Release repressed feelings in a safe and artistic manner.

Steps:

1. Find a paper and pencil and a quiet moment in which to write.
2. Allow lines of nonsequiturs (a statement that does not have to relate to anything previously said) to surface into your mind.
3. Record these as they come in a free verse style.

Variations:

Poems are artistic mirrors of our unconscious selves. They also arise as dreamlike images rife with symbolism, seemingly incomprehensible but full of meaning if we can understand them.

10

Third Person Writing

Goals:

1. Provide an indirect way of getting in touch with buried feelings.
2. Gain insight into repressed material.

Steps:

1. Find a pencil and paper and a few quiet moments to write.
2. Let thoughts arise in any unrelated order and record them like that.
3. Write about yourself in the third person using the pronouns he or she to refer to yourself.

Variations:

Sometimes we can talk "about" ourselves more easily than we can talk "from" ourselves. This exercise can warm us up to talking "from" ourselves by giving us a little distance. As we talk about ourselves our inner image will become clearer and sharper so that we can later address it more directly.

11

Old Rules

Goals:

1. Clarify what we carry in our psyches that has been handed down from our parents.
2. Weed out dysfunctional messages and let them go.
3. Distinguish between our feelings and our parents' feelings.

Steps:

1. At the top of a sheet of paper put your mother's name and father's name or the names of the people who raised you.
2. Beneath each name write whatever adjectives come to mind that apply to these people, such as grouchy, wise, sad, helpful, manipulative and so on.
3. Under this list several unspoken family rules. This means anything that you simply "knew" to do, think or feel, or not to do, think or feel.
4. Go back to your list of adjectives and circle any you feel apply to yourself.
5. Go to your list of rules and circle any that you feel you still live by or pass on.

Variations:

At this point you may do a variety of things. Do whichever of the following applies if you are using this as a personal exercise, homework for group, or in group or workshop.

Discuss with one or two people or the group how you feel these characteristics apply to you and how you feel rules affected you and still do.

Reframe rules into a positive message. "Do not express anger" can be reframed "It is good to express appropriate anger." This exercise was created by Sharon Wegscheider-Cruse.

E X E R C I S E **12**

Family Map

Goals:

1. Clarify family history.
2. Understand the nature of family dysfunction.
3. Place oneself in context.

Steps:

1. On a large piece of paper list your family of origin and your extended family members. List them according to age, with your family of origin at the bottom of the page working up as you go forward in time. Place yourself appropriately. Let it flow loosely and spread all over the paper.
2. Next to each name place the letter or letters appropriate to each.

   A = Alcoholic
   C = Co-dependent
   G = Gambler
   E = Eating disorder

Variations:

You may do this by yourself or with a group. If this is done as a self-help exercise, use it to clarify your own history, to become aware of how much or how little you actually know about your family members and to identify patterns that run from generation to generation. It is also very useful in early stages of group as a way for group members to share history with each other and get comfortable with one another. This exercise was taught to me by Sharon Wegscheider-Cruse.

13

Family Tree

Goals:

1. Gain information and awareness about nuclear and extended family members.
2. Understand the generational nature of family disease.
3. Graph disease pattern.

Steps:

1. Find a large piece of paper and a pencil.
2. Following the general pattern of a family tree or diagram, list as many family members as possible.
3. Place the following symbols next to appropriate names to identify disease patterns within the family:

   A = Alcoholic
   C = Co-dependent
   E = Eating Disorder
   G = Gambler
   W = Workaholic
   D = Divorce

4. Look over your family tree to gain as much perspective as possible on where you came from and where your parents came from.

Variations:

This can be done by an individual as journal work, as take home work brought back to one-to-one therapy or back to the group, or as an exercise in group and then shared with the group. If done in one-to-one or group, discuss them as fully as possible. This exercise helps with parental blame when one realizes that one's parents often grew up in dysfunctional homes as well as one's parents' parents and so on. Dysfunction in these graphs tends to appear like a water balloon, if you press it down in one generation, it swells up in another, or if you press it down on one side of a family, it pops up in another side of that family.

E X E R C I S E **14**

The Shame Pit

Goals:

1. Reduce shame.
2. Understand the difference between chronic shame and embarrassment.

Steps:

1. Find a large piece of paper and a pen or pencil.
2. Draw an abstract image of a pit, reservoir or area of shame that may be within you.
3. Inside of this write a word or phrase about a few pockets of shame that you hide away or store within yourself.
4. Outside of your drawing make little circles or buttons. Next to these write words or phrases that you hear from people that "push a shame button" in you.
5. Connect the "button pushing" phrases with the hidden shame on the inside of your drawing. Notice how a seemingly innocent phrase can so quickly draw you into such a painful place.
6. Share your drawing with another person or with the group.
7. Decide to do something with your drawing either individually or as a group (be creative).

Variations:

As children of dysfunctional "shame-filled" families, we have internalized a lot of chronic embarrassment or shame. Constant embarrassment that had nowhere to go to be safely felt or shared formed an ever increasing pool of paralyzing shame. Just to identify that shame and share it is a powerful experience and helps release some of the toxicity. It's also useful to see how, when you carry this inner pit of shame, even a casual comment can mobilize deeply shameful feelings and have a paralyzing effect. Sharing feelings with others helps reduce this pit. Beneath this shame lies pain and anger so when you begin to release the shame there will be anger and grieving work to do.

15

I Am A Feeling

Goals:

1. Identify subtle negative messages.
2. Provide a safe way to release feelings of inadequacy, anger and negativity.
3. Write one step removed from the first person.

Steps:

1. Do the guided image entitled "Body Voices" (Exercise 96) with your group.
2. With soft background music still playing, ask participants to choose one or two of their negative feelings and write a narrative, as the feeling, telling where you are located in the body and what behavior and feelings you induce. See examples.
3. Share the letters in the group one by one. Just read them and hear them without comment.

Variations:

This can be done after any guided imagery with any feelings. You can also ask participants to journal using this format on their own time.

Examples from clients:

I am *impatience*. I live everywhere in the body. That is, I move around a lot as I am very uncomfortable staying in one place for too long. I know it is better somewhere else and share the statement with Laura all the time. I invade her sense of peace and create dissatisfaction with that moment. I am really very clever in that I can always offer up a basis of comparison which automatically invalidates any positive feeling she might have. I foster agitation by tightening the muscles in her body, by accelerating the heartbeat, by creating a general state of discomfort which leads her to think that she must take immediate action to change her situation. And I always offer up the promise that it's better somewhere else and she should act on that impatience to be in that other place.

I am *guilt*. I live in her forehead and make her run to try to prove that she is good enough. She runs when I call and will jump away from what she's doing and will cook when she doesn't feel like cooking. I also make her hide when she knows she has to do something important. I make her drink coffee on the subway because I know she's afraid she's not going to be ready for her class. I make her run to help friends even though I know she has to take her acting more seriously. I make her work harder and overextend herself at her job; make her afraid to ask for help or admit she can't handle it. I make her ignore her sense of right and wrong and work out the "fair" solution. I make her afraid to put people in their place.

I am *peace*. I live in her stomach. I only come out when she is alone or dancing or acting, when I know people understand what she's trying to say. I come out when she's with Michael sometimes, when he doesn't make demands on her. I also come out at the women's meeting when she feels for someone like Sylvia. I also come out when I know she has loved someone who is no longer around like Joanne and she knows she felt me too.

My name is *anger*. I live in the bowels of her body and I burn holes in her skin. I am secret and powerful and red; I blaze with power and I eat her. I eat the flesh from her bones and I cauterize the wounds. When I have burned away all the pain and the fear, I will be the energy of birth and I will become the flame of protection and I will not ever again go inside and eat my way out.

My name is *grief*. My color is blue. I live behind her jaw and eyes and in her arms. I am more than sadness. I am pain and I am hope. I am the letting go that she can only have by letting me in. I will die only after she lets me live and be. I hurt her and I heal.

29

E X E R C I S E 16

Negative Messages

Goals:

1. Understand the impact of negative messages.
2. Reclaim self by understanding and releasing internalized negative messages.

Steps:

1. Find a large piece of paper and a marker.
2. Either ask a partner to trace around you (beginning at your waist on one side, up over both arms and head and then to your waist and legs on the other side) or draw an outline of yourself on a piece of paper.
3. List all of the negative messages you either have heard or felt growing up or currently at the top of your picture or over your picture. For example, you're clumsy, you're fat, big boys don't cry, etc.
4. Next to each message indicate which person or persons you feel that message may have come from.
5. Share these messages with another person or the group.

Variations:

You may build a sculpture or a psychodrama around where these messages came from and the people involved. Choose people to represent the characters and role play the situation.

You may also wish to write letters to the people you listed telling them how you felt hearing those messages. Release your feelings fully as it is a letter for you alone, or you may wish to write in your journal. Then you can do something with them to symbolically let them go, such as burn them or tear them up while saying the Serenity Prayer. This is an exercise used at ONSITE treatment for co-dependency in Rapid City, South Dakota, and was created by George Bougher, M.Ed., Clinical Director.

17

Inner Face
And Outer Face

Goals:

1. Understand the congruity or lack of it between the outer face or persona and the inner face.
2. Bring this secret information out into the open and share it with others.
3. For the therapist to gain insight into the client.

Steps:

1. Find two fairly large pieces of paper and colored markers.
2. Make two pictures in whatever order you choose. One picture is the person that you present to the outside world, the other is the person underneath the mask. You may add props to your picture if you want.
3. On the side or at the top of each of your pictures write these words then complete the phrase:

> I feel
> I look
> I am
> I need
> I never
> I'm afraid of
> Don't ever call me

4. Share your pictures and anything else you may wish with another person or the group.

Variations:

You may set up a role play with the inner face and the outer face. Have the writer play one face and choose someone to play the other, or have the writer play both roles using two chairs and sitting in a different chair for each role, or set up two chairs and have the writer simply talk to an empty chair with each chair representing a separate face. You may reverse roles if it is helpful.

You may also write a journal entry about these feelings or use the "One-Minute Monologue" (Exercise 44) from the point of view of each face.

This exercise is appropriate for any stage of life: childhood, adolescence, early adulthood or late adulthood.

18

Don't Trust, Don't Talk, Don't Feel

Goals:

1. Get in touch with how dysfunctional family rules were played out in one's family.
2. Understand how these rules continue to play a part in our lives today.

Steps:

1. At the top of a piece of paper write "Past" and underneath write the three column heads of "Don't Trust," "Don't Talk" and "Don't Feel."
2. Under each category list as many ways as you can think of that these rules were in effect and were played out in your family of origin. For example, "Don't Trust" — I never told my sister anything that made me appear weak; "Don't Talk" — I don't remember ever talking to my siblings about Dad's drinking; "Don't Feel" — When Mom screamed at us I hardly heard her, I just snuck away and played quietly in my room or with the dogs. I don't remember crying or admitting to myself or anyone else how much it hurt me.
3. Look over your answers and note which ones still apply to your life today.

34

4. On another piece of paper write "Present" and make the same three column headings. Underneath write how those rules have translated themselves into present-day rules. For instance, "Don't Trust" — I don't tell women in my life anything that would make me appear weak; "Don't Talk" — I don't share my deepest inner hopes, dreams, fears and anxieties easily with my spouse; "Don't Feel" — When something upsetting happens in my life, I don't admit to myself how anxious and hurt I feel. Instead, I go shopping, keep overly busy, work, eat, smoke or use some other way of distracting myself and staying away from the feeling.

Variations:

This is a difficult exercise and will go deeper and deeper as the individual gains more self awareness. It can be done alone or in a group and shared with no one, another safe person or a support or therapy group.

EXERCISE **19**

Role Diagram

Goals:

1. Understand the number and variety of roles played in one's life.
2. Observe those roles in perspective with each other.
3. Set priorities.
4. Gain insight into one's family of origin and the role that one accepted.

Steps:

1. Find a pencil or pen and paper.
2. Make a list of the roles most often played in your life, such as wife, worker (type of work), mother, father, son, daughter, student, writer, chauffeur, social planner, shopper, friend, recovering person and so on.
3. Using circles to represent these roles, draw them as large as they feel in your life (in proportion to each other) and positioned in the order they are played out in your life. The top of the paper will represent those played most often and on down to the bottom as the frequency becomes less. Label the roles.
4. Next to your circles, jot down a few feeling words (angry, happy, sad, etc.) that occur to you as you look at them.
5. Put a plus (+) sign next to the roles that you feel reasonably good about (both the way they feel to you and their relative

size in your life). Place a check (✓) next to the roles about which you feel in some way dissatisfied.

6. After sitting with your chart, take a new piece of paper and draw or list the roles the way you would like them to be in your life.
7. Choose any or all of these roles and do a role analysis on them.

Variations:

On another work sheet list the roles separately. Under each role write a few feeling words that you associate with the roles you play. Also, you can list the amount of time, either in hours per day or hours per week, that you spend in these roles.

E X E R C I S E ## 20

Diagram Of Family Roles

Goals:

1. Clarify the roles played in the family.
2. Gain insight into the family of origin and the role accepted.
3. Gain personal insight.
4. If in a group, share information with other group members both for their insight into the player and for the player to have the opportunity to be heard and seen by the other participants.

Steps:

1. Find a pencil and paper.
2. List these roles:

   A. Addict
   B. Enabler
   C. Hero
   D. Scapegoat
   E. Lost Child
   F. Mascot

3. Next to each role write the name of the person you feel played that role in your family. The roles that family members play can change so you may want to do this exercise two or three times.
4. Compare the lists to see what role you played most often and how the roles did or did not change throughout time.

Variations:

In a dysfunctional family people tend to play rigid roles rather than be themselves and play a variety of roles. There may be a lot of naming and casting people into roles, such as, "Susie's the artistic one," "Danny's the one who always gets in trouble" and so on. The more dysfunctional the family, the more fixed the roles tend to be.

When a child is worried about the behavior of the parents they will often act out to try to take the focus off the failing marriage and onto themselves. Somehow, the natural fear the child experiences in realizing that the people who are supposed to be in charge of his life are incompetent is so great that he would do anything to make his parents look better rather than experience the pain of admitting that his parents are simply not able. The *hero* will work overtime to give the family self-esteem. The *scapegoat* will get into crisis after crisis, diverting the family's attention away from the real problem by giving them something else to worry about. The *lost child* will take care of himself and suffer silently. He will be the child that no one has to worry about — quiet and undemanding. The *mascot* will relieve the tension in the family through clowning, goofing around and so on and will be counted on to perform this function. The *addict* drinks either to kill their own personal pain, because they are an alcoholic personality type and cannot help themselves, or because they feel the basic family disease of co-dependency and do not know how to address their pain openly. The *enabler* will make desperate attempts to keep the addict from using (pouring liquor down the sink, etc.) and to maintain the appearance of a normal, happy family. They will lie to the outside world about what is going on and deny to family members that any problem exists. In a dysfunctional family without drug abuse, the addict may be replaced by a *co-dependent* or two co-dependent parents. The family rules that hold this system together are "Don't Talk," "Don't Trust" and "Don't Feel."

As you can see, each of these roles is vital to maintaining the equilibrium, however sick, of the family system. If one family member stops playing their role, it threatens the entire system. Needless to say, it is wholly against the rules of this family system to recover or get well in any way and if you attempt to break the rules, you will be punished.

21

Role Analysis

Goals:

1. To better understand the roles we play and how we play them.
2. Examine where we are stuck in our roles and where we can exercise choice.

Steps:

1. Choose a role that is important in your life — a primary role such as wife, husband, mother, father, daughter, son, worker and so on.
2. List the people who see you in this role and are a part of the world around the role, namely family, in-laws, co-workers, children, friends, etc.
3. Make seven separate columns with these words at the top: physical, rhythm, taste, smell, texture, psychological, and emotional. List as many adjectives as come to mind in each category, such as, stiff, bent; slow, jerky; bitter, sweet; stinky, floral; rough, wet; crazy-making, supportive; hurting, warm.
4. Make another category called tensions and list the tensions present in the role, for example, financial, power struggles and so on.
5. Make one more category called hungers and list what you hunger for in the role that you don't feel you are getting, such as love, understanding, appreciation, etc.

Variations:

We played many roles in our past, both appropriate and inappropriate, and we do the same in the present. This exercise can be done for any or all of those roles. It can be done for any or several stages of one's life. It can then be shared with no one, a trusted person, a workshop co-participant or a group for discussion and sharing of feelings that arose during the exercise. It can also be a warm-up for experiential work. This exercise was created by Dr. Robert Siroka.

22

Family Role Analysis

Goals:

1. Gain insight into the role played by the participant.
2. Share personal information (if done in a group).
3. Clarify personal history.

Steps:

1. Make sure you have completed "Diagram Of Family Roles."
2. Find a piece of paper and a pen or pencil.
3. Choose the role that you feel you played the most and write it at the top of the page.
4. Make a list of the benefits of the role with the word "Benefits" at the top.
5. Make a list of the liabilities of the role with the word "Liability" at the top.
6. List the situations in which you experience "role leakage" (situations other than your family where you feel you lock into this role).
7. List the payoffs you get from playing this role in and outside the family.
8. List the fears you have in letting go of this role.
9. List the reasons it might be good to continue this role if you so choose.

Variations:

You can take this exercise anywhere you wish. You can make a collage of how you play your role or write a letter from your real self to your role. You can do journal entries about how it felt to play this role, why you did it, your anger about doing it, how you feel it has affected you and why you want to give it up or keep it. In a group situation all of this can be shared with the group.

EXERCISE 23

Family Symbols

Goals:

1. Gain insight into attitudes toward individuals in the family.
2. Gain insight into where family members fit in relationship to you.

Steps:

1. Find a pencil and paper.
2. Close your eyes and imagine yourself and your family members.
3. Think of a different symbol to represent yourself and each of your family members. You may use common symbols such as hearts or stars, animals or famous characters.
4. Place your symbol on the paper then place the other symbols where they seem in relationship to you, using whatever size and distance feels accurate.
5. For each member, including yourself, write a sentence. In the sentence say "I made (name) a _____ because _____" and fill in the blanks.

Variations:

This is good with non-verbal children, adolescents and adults. You may evoke more sharing by asking questions about why they made the choices they made and why they are drawn that particular size and put in that particular situation, after they have shared with you or the group why they have drawn what they have drawn. You may do this exercise twice for addicted family systems: once for the family when there is active abuse and once for the sober family. If extended family members are important they may be included, as well as pets.

E X E R C I S E 24

Psychodramatic Biography

Goals:

1. Write a history that *feels* accurate on a deep level.
2. Gain insight into where your historical truth might differ from your psychodynamic truth.

Steps:

1. Find a pen and paper.
2. Beginning with your birth, write a history that is not actually accurate but reflects the way life felt from the inside out. For example, "I was born on a Greek island in the middle of Minneapolis, Minnesota. We were surrounded by Sweden, Germany and Norway. My father sold fresh fish to these people but always felt like an outsider while my mother mingled with them more freely as she spoke their various languages." Write what it felt like not what it looked like.
3. Share this story with another person or with the group.
4. Tell the person or people you are sharing with why you felt this way after you read your story,

Variations:

You may wish to do this for various stages, such as, birth to adolescence, adolescence to early adulthood, later adulthood, old age. This exercise is inspired by J. L. Moreno's work and the freedom he allowed himself to write his own psychodramatic truth.

E X E R C I S E *25*

Child's Photo

Goals:

1. Gain feeling and historical information relative to childhood.
2. Share this information with other people.

Steps:

1. Find a picture of yourself when you were a child that you feel connected to.
2. Paste the picture in the center of a large piece of paper.
3. All around the paper write the positive qualities, fears, unspoken questions, and insecurities that come up when you look at the picture.
4. Below this write the feelings that were present for this child.
5. In the corner put your childhood nickname.
6. Introduce your child to another person or the group, telling them all that you have written and how you feel about it.

Variation:

You may want to do this for yourself as a child, adolescent, young adult or adult following the same process.

EXERCISE **26**

I Am

Goals:

1. Get in touch with your many facets.
2. Understand the variety of roles you play.
3. Do a fearless moral inventory of all your qualities and accept responsibility for how good you are.

Steps:

1. Read "I Am Maria" silently or to a group.
2. Ask members or yourself to write a similar "I am" history including anything that you might feel like saying with emphasis on personal responsibility and positivity.
3. Share what you have written with another person or the group.

Variations:

You could tailor this to specific needs such as a sober "I Am" and an abusing "I Am." You may do one and put it away, then do another one month later and compare the two.

I Am Maria

Example:

Hi! I'm Maria.

I am Maria and I am intelligent.

I am attractive. I am creative. I am nurturing. I am caring.

Sometimes I'm a caretaker but I'm working on changing that.

I am independent.

I am the child of an alcoholic.

I am a child of war veterans.

I am the grandchild of courageous people.

I am the daughter of immigrants.

I am an American.

I am part South American and part Slavic.

I am organized. I am neat. (Sometimes I am compulsively neat and
   organized.)

I am multilingual. I am creative.

I am a pretty good cook.

Sometimes I am lazy. Sometimes I'm driven.

Sometimes I push myself too hard but I'm working on that, too.

I am sensitive to the needs of others.

Sometimes I'm a good listener. (Sometimes I'm not.)

I am curious. I am spiritual. I am travelled.

I am sensual.

Sometimes I'm powerful. Sometimes I'm powerless.

Sometimes I'm scared.

Sometimes I am very brave.

I have herpes.

Sometimes I feel shame.

Sometimes I feel lonely.

Sometimes I feel inadequate.

I am a woman. I am intuitive.

Sometimes I'm a little girl. Sometimes I'm a woman.

I'm athletic. I am philosophical. I like to write.

I am an aunt. I am a sister. I am a friend.

Sometimes I have a hard time respecting the boundaries of others but
   I'm working on that.

Sometimes I'm tardy. Sometimes I get lost.

Sometimes I feel overwhelmed.

Sometimes I feel sexy.

Sometimes I feel vulnerable.

Sometimes I forget things.

Sometimes I don't know the right thing to say and I get scared.

I am a professional.

Sometimes I feel lonely or vulnerable and I say or do things that I don't like later.

Sometimes I act silly.

Sometimes I behave inappropriately but I'm learning appropriate ways to behave every day.

I am a grateful member of Al-Anon and of an eating disorders group.

I am a former drug abuser.

I am giving. I am generous.

Sometimes I worry what others think of me.

Sometimes I feel ashamed. Sometimes I feel guilty.

Sometimes I feel warm and snugly.

Sometimes I feel threatened and afraid.

Sometimes I feel hurt and angry.

I am a novice skier.

Sometimes I am brave.

I am educated.

I am a product of my past experiences.

I am a fast learner.

I am a survivor of childhood sexual abuse.

I am a victim of incest and rape.

I have a strong will to live. Sometimes I lose that will to live.

Sometimes I am controlling.

Sometimes I feel proud of my accomplishments.

Sometimes I feel inadequate.

Sometimes I feel envy.

Sometimes I feel frustrated.

I am tenacious. Sometimes I am determined.

I am the sister of a homosexual.

I am the granddaughter of nobility.

I am a landlady. I am a tenant.

I am complex. I am a package deal.

I come all wrapped up in many feelings and emotions.

I am Maria and I'm glad to be alive.

I am who I am and I'm glad to meet you.

Who are you?

27

Family Analysis

Goals:

1. Gain information and perspective regarding the family of origin.
2. Gain insight into the relative position of relationships throughout life.

Steps:

1. Find a large piece of paper and something to write with.
2. Divide the paper into four sections using the headings childhood, adolescence, early adulthood, and present.
3. Use the symbol of a triangle for males and a circle for females.
4. In each category place yourself and other members of your family of origin where you felt they were in relationship to you using stick figures. You may include pets, household employees or anyone who actually lived with you during childhood. As a young adult include family of origin members even though you may not live with them.
5. If doing this individually, reflect on it to gain information about yourself and write a few feeling words beside each section describing how you felt during those periods. You may journal about the feelings if you like.
6. If you're in a group, you may also write a few feeling words and then share the feelings you experienced at each stage.

Variation:

Choose any or all of the sections and write a few sentences in the first person about how you felt, who you were, what it was like and so on, then share them with the group.

28

Time Line Family Role Analysis

Goals:

1. Gain insight into oneself.
2. Gain insight into the role you have played.
3. Understand your disease pattern.

Steps:

1. Use a roll of shelf paper and stretch it out across a table or the floor.
2. Begin at the far left end of the paper. Put your birthdate at the top and put the names of the family members who preceded you underneath. Include pictures if you can.
3. On the top half of the paper, from left to right, list any dates that you feel are significant to you and your family, with a brief explanation of what it was. Use pictures wherever possible — births, deaths, marriages, divorces, people leaving home, losses related to family illness, onset of family illness, bottoming out of disease, steps toward recovery, etc.
4. Underneath this list the dates of your personal illness and the use of your survival role or roles. Mark the onset of your disease, its active phase, bottoming out period and steps toward breaking denial and reaching toward recovery. Photos of yourself at these various stages are very helpful.

Variations:

You can use this as the basis for a lot of work since it is your disease pattern and will bring up many feelings. Hopefully, it will also clarify certain things about your life. You can use your journal for writing about feelings that are trigggered, as well as sharing them with another person or in group. You can do letter writing exercises about issues that involve other people in your time line. You can make a picture of the family you did have and the family you did not have, and the role that you learned then and later created in other situations. You can also clarify your own issues about grief and loss, understand what you need to work on or what you need to mourn the loss of and let go.

E X E R C I S E 29

The Empty Chair

Goals:

1. Release feelings toward a particular person in a safe way.
2. Create a situation in which deep feelings can be expressed in a spontaneous fashion thus bypassing intellectual resistance toward the feelings and through the act of spontaneity bring forth more and deeper feelings with less censorship.

Steps:

1. If you are by yourself, set up two chairs facing each other. Sit in one and face the other.
2. If you are in a group, set up the two chairs anywhere where the group can see and hear you.
3. Ask the person doing the work who they have put in the other chair then invite them to say anything they need or want to say to that person.

If you feel they might bring out more feelings and have a greater sense of control by speaking from the other role or get a sense of understanding for the other person, you may ask them to reverse roles. It is important that they actually get up and take the other chair, then speak from that role. They can reverse roles as many times as is appropriate.

4. If this is done in a group, there may be other group members who have strong identification with what is being said by the person working (the protagonist). Invite the people who feel this way to stand behind and slightly to the side of the protagonist and be their "double," saying a few things that they feel further the feeling action of the protagonist. They can stand up and double when it seems appropriate and sit down when it feels appropriate.

5. When you feel the protagonist has spoken fully say, "Say the last thing you need to say" and end the action.

6. In the group share the identification members may feel or what came up for them in watching the action. In this way everyone gets a chance to do personal work and share from their own experience. Keep the sharing on a personal basis; it is not a time for advice giving or questioning. The people who played roles can share from the point of view of the role if they wish.

Variation:

If you do this alone it can be a very relieving personal experience. This is a technique developed by J. L. Moreno, the father of psychodrama and action technique. It was also adopted by and used greatly in the Gestalt movement.

Brief Encounter

Goals:

1. Let out pent-up feelings around a particular incident.
2. Gain insight into each person's point of view.
3. Rewrite history and practice an alternative behavior.

Steps:

1. Ask participants to think of an argument or an encounter with one other person that they found difficult and would like to work with.
2. Set up two chairs.
3. Ask the person doing the work to give a thumbnail sketch of the situation and to briefly describe both people involved.
4. Ask the participant to reenact the encounter saying what they said and then changing chairs and saying the other person's part. They may have to reverse roles many times throughout this process. It is important that they change chairs each time.
5. You may ask for group feedback and sharing.

Variations:

When the participant is setting up the scene, ask them to show you things about themselves and the other person in the situation — show me how this person would sit. How do they hold their body? How do they use their hands?, and so on. It helps warm the person up to the action of talking.

You may wish to give the participant "magic time" and let them do the scene a second time saying and doing what they *wish* had happened in each role, the way they would have liked the encounter to go.

31

Open-Ended Questions

Goals:

1. Let the subconscious answer questions.
2. Gain information.

Steps:

Finish these sentences on separate sheets of paper:

One thing I like about myself is

My favorite treat is

I think it's so cute when

When I was little I liked it when

I feel silly when I

I fear I am inappropriate when

I feel ashamed when I

No one would believe this but

Things would be better if I weren't so

My mother reminds me of a

Every time I hear the word dad I

I feel guilty when I

Lately I've been

It's so sweet when

I feel I barely got through

I'll survive if

I really am great at
Don't even look at me when
I feel all out of control when I
I get so jealous when
I felt especially proud when
I am scared of
Don't ever call me
When I see flowers I think of
The color red makes me think of
Boy, I sure hate it when
If I really thought about it I'd
It always feels so good when
Usually I don't like to
It's funny but
I do
I am

Variation:

This is primarily to gain personal information and spontaneous responses. It may be useful with non-verbal people and young people. You can share the feelings that come up if you choose or journal with them.

E X E R C I S E 32

Social Atom

Goals:

1. For group members to get to know each other.
2. For the therapist to gain insight into group members.
3. Gain insight into oneself and one's life situation.

Steps:

1. Begin with a blank sheet of paper for each person and a pen or pencil.
2. Using circles to represent women and triangles to represent men, ask members to place themselves and anyone they feel is significant in their lives past or present anywhere on the paper in appropriate relationship to themselves and each other. Write in the names.
3. The important consideration in deciding how to put them down is how these people feel to the player rather than how they may or may not actually be in their lives.
4. Anyone who is deceased may be represented using the appropriate symbols only drawing the symbol with a broken line.
5. A member may represent work, pets or any other significant information using the symbols.

6. Let members know that they have about 10 minutes and when they look as if they are finishing, give them a one-minute warning before completion.
7. Invite members to share their social atoms with each other including whatever information they would like about the people on their atom and their relationship to them.

Variations:

This works well for a new group. It helps people get comfortable sharing themselves with others and it gives the group leader much insight into group members.

In reading the social atom look at the way it is organized on the page, where and how the person has placed themselves, relative sizes of symbols, how the person perceives themselves in relationship to others. And any unusual graphics beyond the basic symbolic representation indicates a higher level of anxiety around those people. Does it seem like a reasonably full and balanced atom or is it empty in feeling? How are other people arranged and perceived — are they in their own position or are they clustered and removed? Is there overlapping of symbols with unclear boundaries? Is there an unusual amount of distance between symbols? A group leader should practice doing these on his own and with a few other people before doing it with a group.

Social atoms can be done every six months or so and compared with each other. You may do social atoms for different periods in life, such as childhood, adolescence, early adulthood, adulthood or old age. You may ask people to do a "sober" social atom and a "using or drinking" social atom. This can also be done as a self-help exercise to gain insight into your own social matrix.

This is a technique created by J. L. Moreno as taught by Dr. Robert Siroka.

33

Personal Perception Of Another's Thoughts

Goals:

1. Sort out normal perceptions from distorted ones.
2. Create a sensitivity towards the thoughts and feelings of another person.
3. Allow the player to make the transition from themselves to a character outside themselves by using something more familiar than a character on a page.
4. An exercise in journal writing or in creative writing.

Steps:

1. Pick a person that you know, like your mother, father, sister, brother, teacher, etc.
2. Think of a time when you felt you really knew and understood what that person was feeling.
3. On a piece of paper write exactly what you thought that person was thinking in their mind in the first person.

4. Write a title.

5. If desired, perform this for the group.

Variations:

In dysfunctional homes our perceptions can easily become distorted as we tend to withdraw and try to figure things out in isolation. Because an atmosphere of comfort and trust often is not present in a stressed or traumatized home, we are not able to "check out" our perceptions of a situation with another person in the situation. Furthermore, if we risk doing this we often encounter the denial of other family members who in defense of their need to perceive things as all right or not so bad, will tell us that our perceptions are way off thus making us feel "crazy" and causing us to lose confidence in our way of perceiving things.

This exercise gives players an opportunity to present things as they saw and felt them.

In the classroom this can be used as an exercise in character development. It can be done in reference to the character the child is playing. It can be done along with a history or current events unit as a way of understanding the thoughts of a historical character being studied or a person in the news.

If you have a conflict between children in class, this can be used to role play. The children who are having trouble seeing each other's points of view can write a personal perception of each other's thoughts, then they can exchange and read each other's dialogues followed by a teacher directed discussion. This can also be done in group therapy.

EXERCISE 34

Personal Picture

Goals:

1. Get in touch with the real face beneath the persona.
2. Provide an artistic way of expressing that face.
3. Analyze a face for use in writing or theater.

Steps:

1. Find a piece of paper and some crayons or colored markers.
2. Try to think of how you feel in your mind.
3. Make a picture of yourself from the inside.
4. Use any shapes or colors that you like — you may make a picture of a face or try to draw a picture of your feelings.

Variations:

This could be used in conjunction with a journal; each written entry could be accompanied with a personal picture of the day. If you have a member who is not verbal and you would like more information about them this picture with the personal poem (next exercise) could offer some insights. Also, if the group seems edgy or out of sorts, this can be an effective way of allowing them to express their negative emotions in a creative, non-aggressive way.

This is a way to help the group center itself and you can easily use the picture as a springboard for discussion of moods or feelings after they are completed.

35

Personal Picture Poem

Goals:

1. Provide a way to release pent-up feelings in a safe, artistic manner.
2. Provide stimulation for a writing exercise.
3. Gain insight into character.

Steps:

1. First, draw your personal picture.
2. Now, write a poem to go with the picture.
3. Your poem can be any words or sentences that remind you of your picture or of how you feel.
4. Now copy your poem and put it with your picture, either on the same paper or on another paper.

Variations:

This can be take home work brought back to the group to share. If it is done in the group, some soft music will help people focus.

You might suggest that the poem be inspired by the color of the mood of the picture. It can be a superficial take-off on the way that the picture looks or it can be written in the second person as if about someone else. You may write a poem about how this person does something, such as how they walk, talk, perform a task, etc. There can be several pictures and several poems made into a book.

36

Personal
Picture Story

Goals:

1. Get in touch with the inner child.
2. Give the participant a format to easily bring forth information to be used in a creative writing piece.
3. Beginning character analysis.

Steps:

1. First, make a personal picture of your inner child.
2. Write a little story about the person in the picture.

> A. Give the child's name and age.
> B. Where does the child live?
> C. Who is the child's family?
> D. How does the child feel?
> E. What is the day of this child like?
>
> > 1. Where do they go?
> > 2. What do they do?
> > 3. Who are they with?
>
> F. What does the child do before going to bed?

Variations:

In group therapy you can use this to help people get in touch with their inner child. Allow them to share their stories in pairs along with what comes up for them when they uncover their child. They may also wish to share a couple of sentences with the group on the feelings that arise from this exercise. They will be warmed up if you wish to go on with deeper sharing or experiential work.

In the classroom this is an exercise to challenge the child's imagination and improve creative writing skills. It is also an early step toward creating a performable character either as a part of a larger play or an individual theater piece. You may wish to play music softly while they are working on this.

For a deeper writing experience ask the child to answer these questions or any others that you or he may add to the list: How does the child feel about school, friends, home, activities? What type of child is this? Does this child have outstanding talents or outstanding problems? Explain each characteristic on the picture, namely, hair, eyes and their expressions, mouth and its expressions, etc.

II

Group Exercises

i thank You God for this most amazing
day: for the leaping greenly spirits of trees
and a blue true dream of sky; and for everything
which is natural which is infinite which is yes

(i who have died am alive again today,
and this is the sun's birthday; this is the birth
day of life and of love and wings: and of the gay
great happening illimitably earth)

how should tasting touching hearing seeing
breathing any — lifted from the no
of all nothing — human merely being
doubt unimaginable You?

(now the ears of my ears awake and
now the eyes of my eyes are opened)

e.e. cummings

37

Sculpturing

Goals:

1. Gain information about personal history.
2. Bring on to the "stage" an internal situation and give it three dimensions.
3. Provide an opportunity to work out personal history in the present day with substitute role players.

Steps:

1. Ask the group which one of them would like to work.
2. Ask the person who is working to choose people from the group to play the characters in their personal drama. It may be just one character or it may involve the entire group.
3. Ask the protagonist to tell each person a little bit about themselves to help them to get into the character. Two or three sentences are sufficient.
4. Ask the protagonist what they would like to say to the various characters they have chosen.
5. Allow the protagonist to say anything they like to the characters they have chosen, moving from one to another as they feel so inclined.

6. Allow the characters to speak back to the protagonist if the protagonist desires it. The characters speak as the person they are playing.
7. Let this interchange go on as long as it is constructive and working to get feelings out of the protagonist.
8. When the protagonist seems finished, ask them to say one last thing to each character. Then allow everyone to return to their seats.

Variations:

This is a basic psychodramatic technique and is very powerful. It bypasses much of the intellectualization of talking about oneself and puts one directly into feeling reality, dredging up repressed material from the past that is often a surprise to the protagonist. For this reason it is best to *keep the feedback simple and focused on the people giving it.* Since the protagonist needs support and affirmation for doing this type of work, any critical or negative feedback could be harmful to them in this state.

You may have a group of characters represent one thing that is particularly powerful or significant for the protagonist. It may be helpful to use props to represent things or to help create a character.

Art Game

Goals:

1. Warm up a group to deeper work.
2. Help a new group get to know each other.
3. For the group leader to gain insight into group members.
4. For group members to gain insight into themselves.

Steps:

1. Give each group member two or three large pieces of paper and put boxes of colored pencils or pens around within everyone's reach.

2. On the first piece of paper ask members just to scribble all over to warm them up and lower their inhibitions.

3. Next ask each group member to draw a picture using one of the following ideas or any others:

   A. A place that makes them feel peaceful and happy.
   B. How they would like to be in the future.
   C. A side of themselves that frightens them.
   D. A side of themselves that they feel good about.
   E. What they feel to be a strength.
   F. What they feel to be a weakness.

G. A famous person or character from literature or film that comes into their mind (take the first image).
H. The way they felt at some point in childhood.

4. After everyone has finished with their pictures ask them to share about them, why they drew them and what they mean to them.

Variations:

You may put all of the pictures on the floor and form a loose line, putting pictures that have the same feel to them next to each other and seeing how the group relates to each.

Next ask group members to leave their own pictures and stand behind someone else's picture that they feel connects to them in some way. They can each share why they relate to it. If several people end up grouped behind the same picture they can share common themes. In the case of the picture of a famous person, ask people to talk about what that person may have to say to them. They can put it into one sentence and share it with the group after talking more generally about why they drew it.

This game was inspired by an exercise done by Jean Peterson, C.S.W., T.E.P., A.T.R.

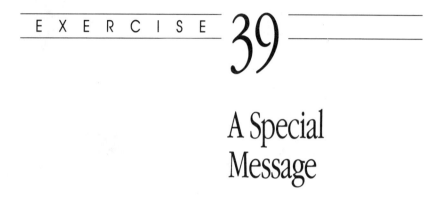

A Special Message

Goals:

1. Get in touch with hidden feelings.
2. Share information with the group and group leader.

Steps:

1. Find a large piece of paper and colored crayons or markers.
2. Ask the group to close their eyes and lead them through a brief centering or relaxation exercise. Use some soft background music or melodic sounds to aid in focusing if you like.
3. Ask the group to allow a character or two from history, literature, television or public life to surface in their minds.
4. Ask them to allow an adjective or two describing these characters to come to mind as well.
5. Now ask them to slowly open their eyes and draw these characters in any form — stick, cartoon or any way — and next to them write the appropriate adjectives.
6. One at a time, ask members to share their picture with the group. They show their picture, say the adjectives, then tell the group what that character might have to tell them personally — a couple of sentences especially for them. After they have said their sentences they may want to share other feelings or thoughts that come up for them.

Variations:

This can be done without using the adjectives or by first listing adjectives, then coming up with a character to represent them. You can also make it more elaborate by using separate pieces of paper and having four to six adjectives and characters, then laying them out on the floor or table in whatever relationship feels appropriate. Ask the drawer to share each drawing separately and then group them together as feels right, telling the group how they relate to each other, what purpose they serve, how the drawer feels about them and so on. After this the entire group can give feedback if desired or if each group member does this you can then see which characters of the group overlap or relate to each other. Then you can bunch them together to form larger groups. Group members can go to whatever group they identify with the most and then share their reasons with the group.

40

Forming
A Family

Goals:

1. Warm up a large group by giving them a common task.
2. Make connections between people in the group.
3. Play out family roles in a variety of ways.
4. Problem solve as a group.

Steps:

1. Ask the group to break up into smaller groups of five or six people.
2. Instruct each member to choose a role in the family such as father, mother, brother, sister, grandparent, aunt, etc.
3. Tell them to begin to interact.
4. After you feel that each character has established himself, give each group a problem to solve. For example, one of you is an addict and needs to be confronted by the family and sent to treatment, find out who it is.
5. Let the groups have five or ten minutes interacting over this until things naturally wind down.
6. Instruct them to bring their interactions to a close.
7. Ask members to share what came up for them in doing this exercise.

Variations:

It is very unlikely that the groups will solve this problem. As in any dysfunctional family, they will project the problem, they will not listen to each other, some will dominate and so on. The objective is not to identify the alcoholic but the symptomatology.

If you are in a small group, you can do this as a warm up to psychodramatic action with one family being played out. This exercise is from a workshop conducted by Robert L. Fuhlrodt, A.C.S.W.

Groups Entertaining The Group

Goals:

1. Problem solve as a group.
2. Encourage creativity.
3. Form bonds within the group.
4. Have fun.

Steps:

1. Ask the group to do a slow walk around the room taking in the room and each person they pass by.
2. Ask them to make eye contact with people as they walk and when they see someone they would like to get to know a little better, join with that person and share a little about themselves.
3. After a minute or two of sharing ask each pair to choose another pair or two who they feel like connecting with and share among themselves. Do this until you have groups of six or eight.
4. Ask each group to find a space in the room and to define it as theirs.
5. Now give each small group the task of occupying or entertaining the large group. Each group shares in whatever way they

choose, by conducting an experiment or a game, creating a story, having a rally, etc. The group leader can check with each group early in the process to make sure that their decisions will be appropriate for the large group.

6. Tell each group they are free to select a leader or two or to operate as a partial or whole group.
7. Give each group the time they need for their piece.
8. After each group has worked leave a little time for sharing at the end.

Variations:

This can be tailored to the needs of a particular group. In business you may wish to give each group business-related problems to solve. Students in the mental health field can solve therapeutic problems and ask the larger group to help in some way. Children in the classroom can use history, for instance, you are a group of cave people looking for a shelter and food supply. How do you organize yourselves, etc.? The goal of bonding and having fun will best be served if you keep it light and give each group as much freedom as possible.

EXERCISE 42

Family Portrait

Goals:

1. Warm up a therapy group.
2. Help a group who may not know each other well share information.
3. For each player to gain clarification about their own situation.
4. For the group leader to obtain quick background information about group members.

Steps:

1. Give each player paper and pencils or whatever you wish to use.
2. Ask each player to draw pictures or stick-like figures of themselves and each member of their family placing everyone on the page in relationship to the drawer and each other as in real life.
3. Have each player explain their drawing to the group and share their feelings about each figure, themselves and how they feel when they look at the picture.

Variations:

Extended family members or close friends, pets and so on can be added to this picture if desired. This can be done every few months to see how things change and it can be done at home to bring to group. People can use crayons, pencils or whatever feels right for them.

E X E R C I S E **43**

Personal Dance

Goals:

1. Use your body.
2. Provide an alternative that involves movement.

Steps:

1. First draw your personal picture.
2. When you look at your picture do you feel like moving?
3. Let your body move however it feels when you think about the picture.
4. If you like you can do your dance to music.
5. Let your personal dance really say what is inside of you.
6. Remember, stillness is a part of dance too so you can use statue or doll images throughout the piece.

Variations:

In general this will work better with children than adults. The adults would need to be a very well-formed group or experienced in movement for this to work, while young children under 10 or 11 years old will find it fun. If they are self-conscious, however, don't push it. Gently bring them back to the floor and do a guided fantasy or read a poem or story.

This is a natural for a performance piece. Ask the child to bring their own music and costume and to do this piece for the class. It can be accompanied with a reading of their poem or their story.

The teacher may want to use a drum to stop the movement periodically and lend structure to the piece. This will greatly reduce self-consciousness on the part of the participants.

There can be a very fruitful discussion after a few children do these for the class. How did they feel about it? What feelings did it bring up? Did they learn things about themselves that were new or put a new light on things they already knew?

EXERCISE 44

One-Minute Monologue

Goals:

1. Gain insight into another person's psychology.
2. Illustrate the difference between how we see someone and how they may see themselves.
3. Stimulate the players' imagination.
4. Provide an alternative to written assignments and create a point of entry into material that can be demonstrated to the group.

Steps:

1. Pick your character. You may choose your character from any-where you like — a play, an historical figure, someone you know, a person on the street or someone from your imagination.
2. Refer to character building exercises and ask yourself those questions about your own character.
3. Prepare a talk of one to three minutes pretending that you are the character. Start out by saying, "My name is *(blank)* and I am *(blank)*."
4. You may bring your own costume and any props you may need and perform this in front of your class.

Variations:

In therapy, a player may play their inner child and speak from that point of view in the first person, or themselves at any point in their life, such as adolescence, during college, while in the army, in the middle of a divorce and so on. They may give a different name to their character even though it is a part of themselves, if they feel it is appropriate.

In the classroom this technique can be used for any individual drama presentation on any subject. It is an easy way to give the children dramatic experience and a sure way of gaining their interest in any subject. This is a one-person theater piece and can be used again and again.

Some subject matter suggestions are an Ice Age person, pioneer, new child from a foreign land, Elizabethan character, Roman character, soldier from a past war, philosopher or actor from the Golden Age of Greece, character from a fairy tale, person from real life they would like to understand better or who interests them.

This exercise will help sharpen imagination and writing skills.

45

One-Minute Imitation Of Another

Goals:

1. Become aware of one's feelings and perceptions about someone else.
2. Learn stage presence and poise.
3. Allow a person to make the transition from themselves to a character outside of themselves by using something more familiar than a character on a page.

Steps:

1. Pick a person that you know like your mother, father, sister, brother, teacher, friend, etc.
2. Think of how that person talks, walks, stands and sits.
3. Write a little one-minute skit imitating that person.
4. Perform your skit for the group or break the main group into smaller groups of three or four and perform it in that group.

Variations:

In therapy this need not be a serious game, it can also be a very comic release of pent-up feelings about a person. Encourage people to be broad in their presentations, using props and costumes if they choose. It can also be a safe way of releasing anger by portraying the person in a negative light or larger than life, as they felt when they were young.

In the classroom this is ideal for bringing acting and play experience into the group without having to mount a production. It also works directly into introducing a curriculum unit and stimulating the child's interest in any subject matter. This is a way of creating a sensitivity in the child, through use of his imagination, either to subject matter from periods in history unrelated to the child's life experience or to a real-life situation that is removed from the child's life pattern.

Refer to "One-Minute Monologue" for further ideas.

E X E R C I S E 46

From Where
I Sit

Goals:

1. Get in touch with the inner child.
2. Recall deep memories from any time in life.
3. Warm up the group.
4. For the group leader to gain information.

Steps:

1. Place a chair facing the group.
2. Invite a member of the group who wants to work to sit in the chair.
3. Ask this person to close their eyes and allow a memory to come forward.
4. Encourage the player to "start in the middle," for example, "I am sitting on the edge of the bed in my room. The bedspread is falling over the edge of the bed and my foot is on it . . ."
5. Allow them to share the memory for several minutes in great detail.

Variations:

Encourage participants to go into very exact detail about their physical surroundings; the greater the detail the more complete the recall. Simply have them describe the situation without any comment on themselves or side coaching from the group leader. They may go into the look on someone's face standing over them, their body position, the sound of their voice and they can say "I am feeling frightened" or "I am feeling good" or whatever, always sharing in the present tense.

This exercise can also be done around specific issues. Refer to the variations in "Sharing A Childhood Memory."

E X E R C I S E  47

Need To Say Game

Goals:

1. Warm up the group.
2. For the group leader to gain information on where each group member "is at."

Steps:

1. Ask each group member to think of what they need to say.
2. Go around the group, each member beginning with "I need to say . . . " and then one sentence related to where they "are at" at this moment.
3. Ask the group members to speak only of their own feeling state and not refer to any other group member.

Variations:

This can also be a one-word "feeling check" by having each member describe their feeling state in one word.

Group members can expand into one to three sentences if the group leader is comfortable with this.

48

Sitting Where?

Goals:

1. Warm up the group and create sensitivity to each other.
2. Share information with the group leader and the other members of the group.

Steps:

1. Allow the group to form naturally and have people sit wherever they choose.
2. When people have settled in, greet them and say a few words of introduction about what you will be doing in the session.
3. Now ask people to notice where they are sitting.
4. Ask people to share how they feel about where they are sitting if any strong feelings come up and if they have any associations or memories that occur to them.
5. Simply take turns sharing these feelings with the group.

Variations:

It is surprising how many feelings can come up in this warm up. Let people elaborate in their sharing. You can use this on its own or in therapy to lead to deeper work with issues that come up. With children it can lead into a discussion of any classroom concern that the teacher may wish to discuss.

After a group has played this game and knows each other well, you may also wish to have members notice *how* they are sitting and share what comes up for them about their body language and how that makes them feel.

I recommend that the group only share about themselves and not offer feedback.

E X E R C I S E  49

Sharing A Childhood Memory

Goals:

1. Warm up each member of the group.
2. Share personal information with the group.
3. For the group leader to gain insight into group members.
4. Get in touch with the inner child.

Steps:

1. Ask each group member to recall a memory from childhood — encourage them to take whatever comes up.
2. Give the group three minutes or so to get into the memory.
3. Go around the group and have each group member share their memory for two to three minutes then, without comment, move on to the next member.

Variations:

When sharing, encourage people to begin in the middle, for instance "I am walking down a road and the smell of dogwood is in the air . . . " or "I am sitting on the floor in the middle of the living room and I hear a crash . . ." This sharing can be done around a topic or an issue such as:

A. Guessing at what normal is (share a memory of a time when you questioned your perception of a situation).
B. A time when you felt very proud of yourself.
C. A time when you felt frightened or unsure.
D. A time when you felt you had tremendous fun.
E. A time when you felt especially close to someone.
F. A time when you felt very much alone or different from other people.

50

House Call

Goals:

1. Get members in touch with early memories.
2. Share information with the group leader and group members.
3. Warm up the group.

Steps:

1. Give each group member a large piece of paper and pencils, crayons, felt tips or whatever you want to work with.
2. Ask each member to close their eyes, relax and recall their childhood home.
3. Ask them to draw a picture of the various rooms, whatever ones they choose to draw.
4. When they are finished, invite them to share about their drawing, how and when they spent time in different rooms, how they felt about it, areas they liked, areas they didn't like and so on, and then share about how they lived in the entire house and how they felt about the rest of the people they lived with.
5. These may be separated into two or more exercises or can be done at the same time.

Variations:

Ask questions about the mood of the house, how it felt to walk in the door, to walk around it, how was space allocated and used by the family. Which rooms did they use, which rooms did they avoid? What were favorite or feared areas and why?

51

Warm-Up Circle

Goals:

1. Establish an affective rapport.
2. Bring the attention of the participants from all of their various preoccupations into the circle with you and onto the work.
3. Create a warm atmosphere, warm them up and prepare them for the work to come.

Steps:

1. Invite participants to join you in a circle on the floor.
2. Take care to make eye contact with the group members and give them a moment to settle in.
3. Ask them to sit up straight, rest their hands on their knees and breathe in a relaxed, even way — you may even want to close your eyes.
4. From here you can begin a simple stretching exercise and allow the group to mirror you. Continue to do this, first sitting then standing if you choose, until you feel that everyone is warmed up and ready to go on to another activity.
5. Quietly give them their instructions for the next activity, such as, "Now turn to the person next to you and get into pairs" or "Now find a space of your own where you can move freely without touching anyone and begin to . . ." etc.

Variations:

A warm-up is a very important part of any creative or therapeutic activity. If you begin every session with this, you will create continuity for your work.

Sit down yourself — never stand and look down at the group while giving them instructions in a warm-up circle. This is a time to establish a calm, creative rapport.

End your session with a circle too. If you want to have a discussion, this is the time to have it. Then thank the participants for their "good work" and tell them that you look forward to the time when you will do this with them again.

A clear beginning and ending to creative work helps adults and children enter into and phase out of the mood.

E X E R C I S E 52

Space Walk

Goals:

1. Develop sensory imagination.
2. Teach people how to put what is in their imagination into physical action.
3. Develop sense memory.

Steps:

1. Begin by walking around the room.
2. Allow your body to relax.
3. Shake out your arms and legs, take a breath and exhale loudly, allowing any tension to leave your body.
4. Let your mind be free of whatever thoughts are in it; let your eyes relax and blur a little, focus on nothing in particular.
5. Allow yourself just to wander around the room with no particular aim.
6. Feel the space around you as you walk, feel the floor beneath your feet, feel the air around you, let your body relax.
7. Continue to walk until you feel an urge to stop.
8. Look straight in front of you.
9. Let your eyes go deeply into what you are looking at.
10. Notice if there is any color, notice the shape and form. Do you think that it is heavy or light?

11. Now begin walking again. Feel a weight on top of your head. Let it go. Feel a weight around your back. Let it go. Feel a weight on top of your feet. Let it go.
12. Continue to walk, taking care not to bump into anyone.
13. Feel the back of your neck. Feel the skin on your arms. Feel your fingers, now stretch them out a little. Feel the backs of your legs. Walk a little more then slowly come to a stop.
14. At this point you may ask the participants to pick a partner to lead into another game.

Variations:

When used as a warm-up activity, have the space walk lead into the next activity. This may mean moving to an area of the room, choosing a partner and so on.

You can experiment with speed during a space walk. Have everyone move at speeds from 1 to 10. When they are moving fast, tell them to move while avoiding touching each other.

In a classroom situation the space walk can also be used as a warm-up activity if done for three or four minutes before another activity.

You can walk through a thicket or a rain forest. It is best to start with a space walk then begin to build a fantasy. Act this out in the first person, such as, you are a character in the Ice Age. Simply talk about the things in the environment. In a walk through the jungle or rain forest you can hear birds and animals, feel sun and rain, walk through gooey mud up to your ankles and so on. Check the guided imageries for ideas on how to talk during a space walk.

E X E R C I S E 53

Finding A Space

Goals:

1. Bring the players' awareness into the room and focus their attention.
2. Define a private, safe space.
3. Help the players get into a creative state of mind.

Steps:

1. Slowly walk or wander around the room.
2. Look for your own space, a space that feels good to you — a space that you would like to be in.
3. Stay in that space and explore it.

    A. Move around the space, notice what is in it. Are there any sounds? Is there a smell or feeling? What is the reach?

    B. Stand up tall and create the limits of your space; your space is as high, wide and low as you can stretch and reach.

    C. Stretch around while standing still and find the limits of your space. Reach high, wide, low and all around. Stretch your legs out and reach with them.

4. Now you know your space. This can be a special space for you any time. You can find a new space to explore next time.

Variations:

This can be used as a warm-up activity or as a transition to rest period. Do this initially without music, slowly, to create a relaxed atmosphere. Next, do this with soft, melodic music that is pleasing to the senses.

Once players have done this several times you can simply put the music on and tell the players to find their space.

Once the players are in their space, they can exercise, relax, do thinking work such as writing a poem or story, go through a relaxation exercise or into a guided fantasy, with or without movement. In therapy you can use a guided fantasy as a warm-up to deeper work (see section on "Guided Imageries"). If you are introducing a new unit, say on Indians, Rome, etc., you may do a guided fantasy to help the child be sensitive to the subject matter.

EXERCISE 54

Mirror Game

Goals:

1. Develop concentration.
2. Develop gross and fine motor control.
3. Develop an ability to work together.

Steps:

1. With a partner, sit or stand facing each other.
2. One of you will start out being the leader.
3. The leader moves very slowly, facing the partner straight on like a mirror.
4. The partner follows exactly what the leader does in every part of their face or body.
5. After a while switch the leader role.
6. After you get used to each other try changing leaders without talking, just by sensing when it is time.
7. When you feel good with that, try having no real leader — just follow each other.

Variations:

1. Three or more members can work together — one leading, two or more following.

2. Encourage members to use their whole bodies.
3. If you are developing or studying characters, all of the movements can be done as the character.
4. If members are working out an issue or issues with a particular person, they can move as that person and be mirrored doing so.

Create a calm atmosphere with this game. Modulate your voice so that it is loud and steady as you give instructions. Create as relaxed an atmosphere as possible as you move the members from activities in pairs to activities with several members, even a circle of 10 or 15 in which they are all following each other. Try to help them deepen their concentration by encouraging them to move slowly without any sound.

55

Pairing
And Sharing

Goals:

1. Establish bonding within the group.
2. Facilitate sociometric choices within the group.

Steps:

1. Ask members to look around the room for a couple of people they feel some connection with and might like to get to know a little better.
2. Invite everyone to stand and take a slow walk around the room making eye contact where they feel comfortable and getting a feel for the group.
3. When they seem ready, tell them to join up with someone and find a comfortable place to sit down together.
4. Ask them to tell each other a little bit about themselves.
5. After they have talked for a few minutes ask them to look at their partner and take in how they are sitting, their point of view and so on.
6. Now ask them to reverse roles and begin talking from the other person's position.
7. After a couple of minutes ask them to reverse back. You may reverse roles more than once.

8. With your partner, move back into the larger group and share your experience.

Variation:

You may wish to have one pair seek out another pair or two, if the group is large, and share their experience in that way.

EXERCISE 56

Personal Sharing

Goals:

1. Warm up and mix up a group.
2. Share something personal in a game-like way.
3. Help the group begin to network.

Steps:

1. Form two circles equal in number, one inside the other.
2. Play some music and ask both circles to walk around in opposite directions from each other.
3. Tell the players that when the music stops they should stop and face the person they are opposite in the other circle.
4. Ask them to say, "One thing I would like to work on here is . . ." then finish the sentence. Designate which circle, inner or outer, shares first and which circle shares second.
5. Start the music up again and go through the same process, changing what they share each time (see variations).
6. On the last time have the members form pairs or small groups, go to a separate area in the room and share with each other what they would like to work on about themselves and anything else around that they choose.

112

Variations:

Partners can share anything that you feel is appropriate to the work you are doing. Here are a few suggestions:

1. One thing I hide from other people that I like about myself is
2. One thing I hide from other people that I don't like about myself is
3. I consider one of my strongest areas to be
4. I consider one of my weakest areas to be
5. One thing I love to do is
6. One thing I hate to do is
7. One of my favorite relatives is
8. One of my least favorite relatives is
9. One positive message I remember from childhood is
10. One negative message I remember from childhood is
11. My favorite color is
12. My lucky number is
13. My nickname or the name I like to be called is
14. A name people have called me that I didn't like is
15. A show business person I admire is
16. A show business person I do not like is

Another variation is if you stop the circle in pairs you may use it as a lead-in to mirror exercises, if you would like a quieter, non-verbal atmosphere.

E X E R C I S E 57

Doll Game

Goals:

1. Develop presence and concentration.
2. Teach members to maintain their body position while being watched.
3. Practice physical control.
4. Physicalize internal issues.
5. Provide a lead-in to deeper emotional work.

Steps:

1. Find a friend to play this game with.
2. Decide who will be the doll and who will be the dollmaker.
3. The person playing the doll should sit in a completely flopped over, rag doll position.
4. The dollmaker moves the doll into a pose — moves the arms, legs, head, face, mouth, fingers, hands, etc., into a pose. Make sure that it is a pose that is easy to hold.
5. Now look at the doll you have made.
6. Next switch places, the doll becomes the dollmaker and the dollmaker becomes the doll.
7. You can play this in a small group with the doll in the middle of a circle and two or three friends looking on.

114

Variations:

This could be a charming and simple theater piece if you let all the members be dolls in a toy shop. Have one toymaker who walks into the shop and turns on the light and the music and one at a time winds up the dolls. The dolls come to life and can do a movement or dance. Then they wind down or run out of steam.

The members could either make their own costumes for this or you could have a large costume box. The theater piece could be accompanied by one child reading a story about anything — a fairy tale, an Indian village, a Halloween night, etc. Each individual could also be given one or two lines or a short poem to recite.

58

Emotional
Doll Game

Goals:

1. Develop a sensitivity among the members for each other's emotions.
2. Give the members an artistic form for expressing feelings.
3. Teach performance and stage readiness.

Steps:

1. Ask members to work in pairs.
2. Each pair thinks of an emotion.
3. One of the members will be the dollmaker and the other one will be the doll. The doll will lie in a flopped over position, like a Raggedy Ann waiting to be posed.
4. The dollmaker will put the doll into a comfortable position the doll can hold, that expresses the emotion that they have chosen. Don't forget to form an appropriate expression on the face.
5. The other members can now guess which emotion the doll is expressing.

Variations:

Encourage the members to hold the position exactly as they are posed and make sure the dollmaker puts them in positions they can hold.

You may do it relating to personal or family feelings. You may also assign roles and have one dollmaker put several dolls into position surrounding a specific issue. For example, when someone yells at you, put the dolls into position showing how you feel when that happens.

If you are in the classroom studying a unit on settling in America, you might do this game to help the children become involved with how people felt about that experience.

E X E R C I S E 59

Doll-Making Game

Goals:

1. Clarify the player's feelings about the doll character.
2. Share information with the group.
3. Provide a non-threatening warm-up to more direct action.

Steps:

1. Ask members to work in pairs.
2. Each pair thinks of an emotion.
3. One of the members will be the dollmaker and the other one will be the doll. The doll will lie in a flopped position, like a Raggedy Ann waiting to be formed.
4. The dollmaker will put the doll into a comfortable position the doll can hold, expressing the emotion they have chosen. Don't forget to form an appropriate expression on the face.
5. The other members can now guess what emotion the doll is portraying.
6. Have the player give the doll the name of a person he would like to say something to.
7. Have the player tell the doll about this person. "You are . . ." etc.

8. Have the player tell the doll how he feels about them. Encourage the player to speak openly to the doll saying whatever comes to mind.
9. The doll does not respond.
10. If the player desires a response from the doll he can pull a string at the back of the doll. When he wants the doll to stop he can pull the string again.
11. The doll always responds in the first person from the point of view of the character being portrayed.

Variations:

You may add music, costume pieces or props if it enhances the mood. After the piece is finished, invite other group members to share with either the doll or the player saying "Dear so and so, I feel . . ." and so on. Keep each individual sharing for one or two more minutes. Group members may also wish to share what came up for them when they watched.

EXERCISE 60

Family Doll Game

Goals:

1. Clarify the player's feelings about the doll character.
2. Share information with the group.

Steps:

1. Choose a player who is interested in telling a story.
2. Have her assign family member roles (mother, brother, etc.) to as many players as necessary. The entire family need not be portrayed.
3. Have the lead player position each doll in relation to one another in a large playing area.
4. Ask the lead player to put each doll into a body pose appropriate to their character and to tell them a little bit about themselves in two to three sentences.
5. Now let the lead player talk to each character and say whatever they need or want to say (the therapist or teacher may wish to stay next to the lead player for support).
6. If the lead player would like any doll to respond, they may pull the string at the doll's back and when they want them to stop they may pull the string again or ask the therapist to do so.
7. The doll always responds in the first person from the point of view of the doll's character.

120

Variations:

You may wish to have "magic time" here for the lead player. In this case the lead player would say "magic time" to the doll and the doll would say all of the things the lead player might wish they had heard from the character being portrayed, for example, "You were always so kind and I enjoyed you so much . . ." and so on.

61

Family Role Doll Game

Goals:

1. To understand better how the roles of an addicted family were played out in their family of origin.
2. Clarify the player's feelings about the doll characters.
3. Share information with the group.

Steps:

1. Ask for a volunteer to tell a story and others to assist.
2. Ask the lead player to assign the roles of Addict, Enabler, Hero, Scapegoat, Lost Child and Mascot to the other players.
3. Have the lead player tell each player their name and two or three sentences about how they played their role. The lead player positions each doll around the space in relation to each other.
4. Next, ask the lead player to put each doll into the appropriate body position. They may continue their character description as they do this if they choose, but briefly.
5. Now let the lead player talk to each character and say whatever they need or want to say (the therapist or teacher may wish to stay next to the lead player for support).
6. If the lead player would like any doll to respond, they may pull the string at the doll's back and when they want them to stop they may pull the string again or ask the therapist to do so.

7. The doll always responds in the first person from the point of view of the doll's character.

Variations:

You may wish to have "magic time" here for the lead player. In this case the lead player would say "magic time" to the doll and it would signal the doll to say all of the things the lead player might wish they would have heard from the character being portrayed, such as, "You were always so kind and I enjoyed you so much . . . " and so on.

E X E R C I S E 62

The Cocktail Party

Goals:

1. Create a group spirit.
2. Bring unconscious feelings to conscious level.
3. Act out and raise the awareness level of real feelings in a situation.

Steps:

1. Invite the group to attend a cocktail party.
2. Allow everyone to choose a role (they need not tell the group what they have chosen). There will be guests, waiters, waitresses, hosts and so on.
3. Signal that the party has begun and ask players to begin acting out their roles; they can talk and move about freely.
4. After a couple of minutes, when the party is going well, say "FREEZE."
5. Now ask players to act out the inner life of their character, saying and doing what is really going on inside.
6. Next say "go back to the party" and ask them to return to the party.
7. Repeat this as many times as you desire.
8. You may "unfreeze" one character at a time and question them about their inner life if you wish.

Variations:

Music can be used to help create an atmosphere, as well as costumes and props. After this game people will have feelings that they will want to share. Discuss what came up for everyone.

Pretend you have a microphone when the group is frozen and go up to any member of the group. Invite them to speak into the "mike" using their character voice in the first person and to talk about what is going on with them.

Another fun way to play this game was created by Bill Maloney, M.S.W. Have group members write on a piece of paper several inappropriate party behaviors such as standing too close, bragging, hands all over someone, talking someone into a corner, looking at everyone else in the room while carrying on a conversation with someone, talking too loud, staring at the floor while talking, playing with one's own hair or clothes, creating long uncomfortable pauses before and after speaking and so on. Have each member pick one behavior out of a hat and act it out at the cocktail party. After a few minutes of this you can freeze action (microphone can be used here if desired). Later you can "unfreeze" and go to acceptable party behavior. You can switch back and forth and then share what comes up for people in the group.

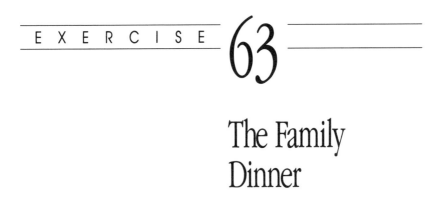

E X E R C I S E **63**

The Family Dinner

Goals:

1. Create a group spirit.
2. Bring unconscious feelings to conscious level.
3. Act out and raise the awareness level of real feelings in situations.

Steps:

1. Invite the group to a family dinner of any size that you choose. It can be a nuclear or an extended family.
2. Ask each group member to assume a role (mother, brother, aunt, grandfather) and to share it with the group so that the roles are appropriate to a family. Servants may be added if appropriate.
3. Seat the family members at the dinner table.
4. Tell them that dinner has begun and ask them to begin to interact.
5. When things are moving along say "FREEZE" and then instruct the players to act out the inner life of their character.
6. Then tell them to go back to the dinner and their outer character.
7. Repeat this process as often as you like until the game is over.

Variations:

This game can be played using Sharon Wegscheider-Cruse's roles of Alcoholic, Enabler, Hero, Scapegoat, Lost Child and Mascot for much added depth. If you use these roles the players will want to share what comes up for them after the game is over.

While you have the characters frozen you can go around to the various characters and ask them to speak into the microphone and share what is going on with their inner character then resume the scene and repeat.

EXERCISE 64

Building A Story

Goals:

1. Warm up the group to personal issues.
2. Break through the barrier of plot creation in story writing.
3. Give the players an easy and cooperative way to build an imaginary situation.
4. Give the players an imaginative way to explore alternative choices.

Steps:

1. Invite players to sit in a circle.
2. Begin a story by having any member say one sentence.
3. Going clockwise around the circle, each member repeats all that has been said and then adds on a sentence.

Variations:

This is a game to get the players' creative juices flowing to do theater or creative writing. If you stop the story before the end, you can ask the players to write the story out and add their own ending.

To start a therapy group you may wish to ask if any group member has a particular issue in mind and begin the story around that issue. This will bring to the surface the group's feelings about the subject and allow them to share with each other in a less personalized way while having fun creating the story.

65

Mood Name Tags

Goals:

1. Warm up a large group.
2. Get people talking about feelings.

Steps:

1. As people enter the room give them a mood tag rather than a name tag.
2. Ask them to write in one or more words their mood at that moment.
3. Invite them to enter the room.
4. Participants may wish to ask other people about their mood or share their own mood with someone.
5. You may simply leave the warm-up at this or you can go on to form mood groups.
6. If you form mood groups check the various moods and group them together as feels right. There may be isolates whose mood doesn't seem to fit any group.
7. Let the groups share among themselves
8. Move back into the larger group and let anyone who would like to share in the larger group do so. This can move naturally into action or remain verbal sharing.

Variations:

You can put other things on the tag as well, such as secret wish, hidden fear, profession you wanted to be when you "grew up," your least favorite characteristic in other people, what you secretly wish you did for a living, what you would name yourself if you could have another name, a characteristic about yourself that you try to hide from other people, the thing about yourself that you are most proud of, the thing you are the most embarrassed about, your favorite thing about yourself as a child and so on, then follow the same procedure (use this with a group that knows one another fairly well).

EXERCISE *66*

Build A Machine

Goals:

1. Create a group rapport and esprit.
2. Learn cooperation.

Steps:

1. Ask one player to begin a motion that is machine-like, such as moving an arm up and down.
2. Ask the next player to add a movement that adds to the machine and corresponds to the movement that player #1 is making.
3. Ask the third player to add a movement that corresponds to player #2 and so on until you have built an entire machine.

Variations:

You can have each part add a sound to their movement which makes the machine more expressive. You can vary the feeling of the movements from staccato-like to fluid and graceful. You can direct any one part of the machine to speed up and slow down on a scale from 1 to 10 and have the rest of the machine figure out what the new speed is and try to adjust to it.

EXERCISE 67

Build A Dysfunctional Machine

(Do this after "Building A Machine.")

Goals:

1. Illustrate the strain present in a dysfunctional family that is not operative in a normal family.
2. Create rapport and esprit.
3. Learn cooperation.

Steps:

1. Ask one player to begin a motion that is machine-like, such as moving an arm up and down.
2. Ask the next player to add a movement that adds to the machine and corresponds to the movement that player #1 is making.
3. Ask the third player to add a movement that corresponds to player #2 and so on until you have built an entire machine.
4. Ask the original part of the machine to suddenly change its movement.
5. Instruct the rest of the machine to change its movement correspondingly.

6. Once the machine adjusts go back to the original player and instruct him to suddenly change his movement again.
7. Instruct the rest of the machine to change.
8. Do this several times.

Variations:

You can add sound to this to create a richer, more complicated machine. Here the discussion is crucial. Ask group members how it felt to be part of a machine that continually changes its function and is unpredictable.

E X E R C I S E *68*

Picture Game

Goals:

1. Develop a critical eye.
2. Develop presence.
3. Develop stage sense; that is, how to create physical images on stage.
4. Create a sense of fun and playing around the art of performing.
5. Become comfortable moving in unusual ways.

Steps:

1. Define an area of the room as the picture area.
2. Go to the other side of the room with the group.
3. One by one tap the members as they move to the picture area and immediately freeze into a shape. Five to a picture is plenty.
4. Emphasize that they are making a picture together and, as each new member enters, they should build on what is already there in some interesting ways — even to go directly across or opposite, as long as it is in spatial relationship.
5. Let the other members observe the picture. Other members can pretend to be artists and find a favorite view or angle from which to paint a picture of the sculpture.

Variations:

This game helps people follow directions and develops stage presence. Members need to remain frozen while taking part in a picture. Children love this game and can do it virtually endlessly.

It is a good game to start out with because it is easy, active and to the point. When the members run up to take their place, encourage them to get in instantly, with no extra movement before they freeze into position, and to take a shape that complements what is already in the picture.

E X E R C I S E **69**

Musical Chairs

Goals:

1. Create a lively group energy.
2. Play and have fun.

Steps:

1. Count the number of players in your group.
2. Subtract one from that number and place that many chairs back-to-back in the center of the room.
3. Ask everyone to walk around the chairs while you play music and to immediately sit down when the music stops.
4. There will be one player who does not have a chair and that player will watch from that point on.
5. Remove another chair and repeat these steps until there is only one person left in the game.

Variations:

This game is great for breaking down barriers and just having a good time. I always play to win but, for some reason, have just as much fun losing and cheering everyone else on.

If you wish, you may share feelings that come up in the group members during the game around winning, losing, having fun, being in, being out and so on.

EXERCISE 70

Follow The Leader

Goals:

1. Warm up a group and create rapport.
2. Stimulate the imagination in a particular area of interest.
3. To help make a study subject seem real in the classroom.

Steps:

1. Begin with one leader.
2. Decide your area of interest or emphasis. The leader begins moving, for instance, walking like an Indian in the classroom or a person who is drunk in therapy.
3. All of the members follow the leader and do just as he does — use all the space you have.
4. Change leaders whenever you feel it is appropriate until the game is over.

Variations:

This is an all-purpose cornerstone game for the classroom. If it is Halloween, the leader can be a witch. If it is history, the leader can be an Indian or a pirate and if it is science, the leader can be a reptile.

This game is one that can be used in literally any situation. It is great for character development because it helps the children give their character physical life. It is a good warm-up because it loosens the child up and gets them concentrating on physical shapes. It is very important for a child to physicalize a character — to give it a physical life, a body and a shape. For a child this is probably the most important aspect of character development. You can also play "Follow The Leader" giving the character a voice, the next step for a child in developing a character.

Use this also just to play. Change leaders and let the children lead either in play or character development exercises.

If you want to lead into deeper work, have members physicalize and lead the group as people with whom they have issues and have the entire group follow them.

71

Statue Game

Goals:

1. Increase physical coordination, movement and concentration.
2. Introduce any unit of study in a fun, game-like way.
3. Stimulate imaginative interest in a particular area of study.

Steps:

1. Ask the players to spread out so they can each have comfortable space to work in.
2. Explain to them that every time you hit a beat, they go into a frozen position. They change position on each new beat. The idea is to change as soon as they hear the beat and freeze immediately. A drum is the best and most distinctive beat, if you have one.
3. Remind the players to use facial expressions appropriate to the physical statue.

Variations:

This is an all-purpose cornerstone game. It can be done just as a pure game to enhance movement, coordination and concentration or you can do the game in any character, such as statues of war characters, statues of Christmas characters, statues of animals, etc.

In therapy you can announce a mood such as happy, depressed, mad, angry, peaceful and so on, either on each clap or every few claps, to physicalize the mood.

You can use this in conjunction with the "Emotional Doll Game" around the theme already assigned. It can help players identify and explore their own emotional reactions and learn about them.

If you are doing a play with children and want to help them develop character attitudes and poses, this game is a must. It is a short cut to character building and since children respond better to impulse, you will get farther than if you explain and intellectualize about a character. Also just do this for fun with no particular theme. Remind them to use their facial expressions.

Blind Walk

Goals:

1. Develop tactile sensitivity by isolating one sense.
2. Learn to trust a partner.
3. Introduce creative writing.

Steps:

1. Find a friend to work with.
2. Ask this friend to close their eyes tightly or put a blindfold on them.
3. Stay in one place and give your friend things to touch and put their hands on.
4. Walk slowly around the room letting your friend touch and feel anything.
5. After you have finished switch places, so that the person who was blindfolded becomes the person who is leading.
6. Talk about what it felt like to only have the sense of touch with no sight.

Variations:

This game develops a feeling of closeness between the partners. After the game, for which you should allow plenty of time, invite the players to work in their pairs or two pairs to join together and write some free associations — maybe 10 words about what it felt like to be without sight. Let them talk among themselves about how it felt, then write a little story or poem called "I Felt," talking about how their environment felt and appeared to them through only the sense of touch.

73

Hearing And Sensing Game

Goals:

1. Isolate the hearing sense and sharpen it.
2. Create environmental sensitivity.
3. Have fun cooperating.

Steps:

1. Ask the players to sit in a circle.
2. Two players go into the center of the circle and sit with their backs against each other and eyes closed or blindfolded.
3. One player from the circle creeps toward the players in the center.
4. The players in the center try to sense the direction from which the person is approaching and point at them.
5. Once they sense where the person is approaching from, that person sits down and another person begins to approach. Do this as many times as you like then change the players in the middle.

Variations:

You can vary the game by allowing the players to sit anywhere in the room. Have one person in the middle of the room standing up with a blindfold on or sitting on a desk or chair. The teacher points to people at various locations in the room, each person makes a quiet sound of one kind or another and the person in the middle of the room points in the direction they think it is coming from.

Have all the players just sit in a circle and listen. Talk about what sounds you hear that you are not normally aware of.

E X E R C I S E 74

Freeze Photo

Goals:

1. Help people show feelings with body movement.
2. Learn to express feelings creatively.
3. Begin to analyze body language. This is beginning character analysis.

Steps:

1. Find a partner.
2. The two of you pick an emotion.
3. Think of a way to show that emotion by the way you position your body.
4. Both of you take a position to show the emotion.
5. Ask your friends to guess which emotion you're trying to show.

Variations:

If you have anything you would like to talk about with the group, this could be a way to lead into it. The members can talk about the emotion they are expressing and those looking on can talk about how they feel.

This can be a creative release and tool for expressing certain emotions safely without feeling put on the spot.

Note — no cross-talk. A player may only say how they feel when they do an emotion or how it makes them feel (in the first person) when they look at someone else's picture. This is not a comment on the picture. It is a reflection of the feeling that it evoked in the viewer.

E X E R C I S E 75

Emotional Still —
Sound — Words

Goals:

1. Learn to add words and sound to the physical character already established.
2. Develop a sensitivity among the group for each other's emotions.
3. Give the group members an artistic form for expressing feelings.
4. Teach performance and stage readiness.

Steps:

1. Find a partner.
2. Decide with your partner what emotion you would like to show.
3. First, pick a still body pose that you feel expresses that emotion.
4. Take that position and hold for several counts.
5. Now add a sound that you feel expresses that emotion. You can make the sound at the same time, take turns or make a pattern by one person making the sound a few times then the other person, etc.
6. Next add a word(s) that you feel is close to the emotion and use the word(s) in the same way that you used the sound.

Variations:

This is the beginning of playwriting and you will be amazed by what both adults and children come up with. You can spend a lot of time with this activity, giving the players plenty of time to create their scene. Build up slowly. At first give them just a couple of minutes, but when they get the hang of it they can almost write little scenes in their minds and perform them for the group as vignettes. If you like, they can eventually write these down as small scripts and perform them as theater pieces with costumes, props, music or whatever seems appropriate.

76

Pin The Emotion On The Person

Goals:

1. Develop a sensitivity among the group for each other's emotions.
2. Give the players an artistic form for expressing feelings.
3. Teach performance and stage readiness.
4. Have fun cooperating.

Steps:

1. Ask one player to act out an emotion.
2. Ask the other players to guess what the emotion is.

Variations:

1. More than one child can do the acting.
2. The acting out can be dramatic or it can be a frozen picture of an emotion.

You will be surprised at how poetic some of these little scenes will look and how much emotion they will convey. In developing a character or a mood on stage, one needs to use this sort of technique to set the tone of the play and this is a very simple way for the players to learn how to develop that type of stage power. They will also surprise themselves at how a frozen scene can show so much.

If you like, you can have a discussion after this on creating stage emotion and mood, or you can veer off into how we show our feelings through our bodies and how we affect and understand each other on a non-verbal level.

77

Charades

Goals:

1. Develop a sensitivity among the group members for each other's emotions.
2. Give the group members an artistic form for expressing feelings.
3. Become comfortable showing feelings.
4. Teach performance and stage readiness.
5. Have fun cooperating.

Steps:

1. One player acts out something specific, such as pretending to be a certain animal or person or pretending to be doing a certain activity such as sewing, playing cards, watching and so on.
2. The other players try to guess who the acting player is or what they are doing.
3. You can have players working together in twos, threes or fours miming a situation or an activity while the others guess.

Variations:

The variations on this game are as many as you can dream up. The game can be played by one player, two, a group or teams.

You may wish to play "Feeling Charades" by writing an assortment of feelings on scraps of paper to put into the hat and have members draw a feeling and act it out. You may also have each member think of one quality that they are afraid people will see in them and they feel self-conscious or ashamed about and another quality that they feel especially good about and wish people would notice and act each of these out. They need not be done at the same time.

In classroom, for subjects like history or current events, you can mime, for instance, all the activities from the Ice Age or cave man's time or ancient Greece, Rome, Pompeii, etc.

78

Caught In A Lie — Talk Your Way Out

Goals:

1. Give the players the opportunity to get in touch with the process of lying and its consequences, in a safe and playful manner.
2. Enhance stage-drama awareness.

Steps:

1. Think of a situation when you have done something that you were not supposed to do or felt ashamed about something you did and you lied about it.
2. Have a partner ask you questions about what you were supposed to be doing.
3. You must say anything you can to avoid telling the truth.
4. After you finish this exercise discuss it. What did it feel like to be caught in a lie? How does it make a person think when he is lying? How does it make a person act when he is lying?

Variations:

Morality is the subject here. This exercise gives the players a chance to bring lying out of the shadows and into the group activities where they can really see it. It gives them a chance to establish what lying is and to experience it through drama, to see the bind that it puts them in.

The discussion is an important part of the exercise. In *Adult Children of Alcoholics* Woititz says, "Adult children lie when it would be easier to tell the truth." This game works with that concept. This game was created by Marina Dayton.

79

Frozen Scene

Goals:

1. Warm up the group.
2. Learn poise.
3. In the classroom, to introduce any unit of study and to help make it real and current for the children, as well as fun.

Steps:

1. Ask two of the players to be the directors.
2. Choose a situation from any subject. Pilgrims landing on shore, observed by Indians; a royal court; cave men and women; working animals or wild animals and so on.
3. Ask the directors to put the actors into their positions and ask the actors to freeze these positions. It is best not to use more actors than can concentrate all at once.
4. Repeat several times around the same theme.

Variations:

After this exercise you can ask the players to write some dialogue or a one-act play about what happens to the characters. Then the players can perform it for the group.

This can also be used as a light warm-up by having two or three group members make the scene and other members share what comes up for them with the group or write it in their journal.

80

Acting Out Stories

Goals:

1. This can be a warm-up for the inner child. You can choose provocative children's literature or poetry.
2. This is useful in dramatizing any unit of study. Introduce the unit in this manner.
3. In the classroom, renew the children's interest in a long unit by using this at a mid-point.

Steps:

1. Choose a story to read aloud. This story can be from history or current events. It can be a science story about how a flower or a bacteria grows, it can be about how a wolf pack socializes or how a bear prepares for hibernation. This exercise is a cornerstone activity that can kick off any unit of study.
2. Ask the players to lie quietly on their backs with their eyes closed while you read. At some point you tell them to begin moving to the story that they hear. It is not necessary for them to take parts unless you want them to. They can simply act out what they hear as they hear it. The purpose is to get their imaginations going about a particular subject so they will more readily internalize the information. If you would like to have music playing in the background, that can help focus their

attention and will help them ignore small distractions in the environment. Try this once, it is surprisingly easy.

Variations:

In the classroom you can create any atmosphere you wish with this activity. If you are studying photosynthesis, you can talk the children through the growth of a seed to a plant while they move to your words. They will understand the concepts much more clearly if they physicalize them.

If you are studying a unit on prehistoric man, talk the children through a situation in the life of early man while they act it out. Choose something simple like making tools, hunting for food and roots, making a cave area, starting a fire and cooking food or whatever appeals to you.

You can begin by inviting them to go to "their space" or anywhere in the room. Talk them through a relaxation exercise and then begin to talk about the subject of your choice. They will all move around the room to your words, miming the activity that you narrate. At the end of the narration bring them slowly back to their space. You can use "I Am A Rainbow" as a general pattern to follow and you can do "Finding A Space" a few times to get the children used to this way of working. You can make time lines to follow up this activity.

Always begin by having the children lie on the floor for a brief relaxation to get them to mentally disengage from their previous activities and go more fully into this one. Create a calm, relaxed atmosphere if you want this to work well.

E X E R C I S E

EXERCISE 81

Individualized Theater Piece

Goals:

1. Gain insight into someone and share information with the group and leader.
2. Provide an alternative to a written report.
3. Develop research skills.
4. Develop script writing skills.
5. Provide stage experience.

Steps:

1. Members may wish to use their character from "Inner Face And Outer Face" or choose a new person.
2. In the classroom you may assign a character or allow the player to choose a historical character to research.
3. As with a written report, proceed with regular steps to research the character's life and times.
4. Ask the player to write the information in the first person talking about themselves, their personal lives, the times they live in and what they feel they have contributed or hope to contribute.
5. Present this to the group, allowing the player to use props, costumes, music or anything that seems appropriate.

Variations:

In group therapy, members may wish to share with the presenter after their piece. They should share in the first person (no advice) and they can frame their sharing as a letter, for example, Dear (name of character), . . . Love or From or any appropriate closing and their name.

In the classroom, rather than reporting only on famous people the player might choose to be the child of a famous person, talking about them from that point of view or simply any child at any period in history. In this case the presentation can be more of a personal view of a given period in history.

For example, a child in the Ice Age could talk about what their day is like, what survival skills they learn, their living situation and how they survive the winter with the clan. Props could be rough tools, animal skins, special stones and so on. This can be done for virtually any period from a child's point of view.

III

Guided Imagery

"Our palate for the taste of life has become numb because we have forgotten how to dream . . ."

from *Going Within*
by Shirley MacLaine

82

Taking Care Of The Child Within

A Guided Imagery To Reparent The Inner Child

(Speak aloud slowly to an individual or group or onto a cassette tape.)

Sit in a comfortable position or lie on your back with your palms facing the ceiling. Mentally move through your body and locate any tension that may be present, any areas where your muscles are holding an uncomfortable position, and ask your mind to ask your body to relax. Simply let go. With each breath go deeper into a state of relaxation, breathing in quiet and relaxation and breathing out anxiety and frustration. In your mind allow an image of yourself as a child to arise. Any age that comes to mind is good. Look at the child in your mind. Look at the hair, the eyes, the mouth, the expression, the clothes, the body position; take in all of your child. That child wants something from you, something that you are able to give. You are going to stand up and put your child in the chair where you were sitting. It is very important that you actually physically get up and put your child where you were. Go ahead and do that now. Good. Look at your child. Your child needs something from you. Now it's time to give that child what it needs — whatever it is asking for give freely. Now it's time to physically take care of your child. Take the time that you need now to do for your child. Look at that child and love that child. Your child needs something from you that you are giving it now.

Take some time to nurture and give to your child. (At this point allow a couple of minutes for participants to continue to take care of their inner child. You may wish to play some very soft music. When people seem to be finishing begin with the next line.) Whenever you feel ready, do the last things you need to do or whisper the last things you need to say to your child. Let your child know that it is safe and that you will be back to visit again. Slowly allow your attention to return to the room and whenever you feel ready you may open your eyes.

This is a guided imagery I learned from Zerka Moreno, the doyenne of psychodrama and the wife of J. L. Moreno, the father of psychodrama and action technique.

83

Turning Over
A Desire

A Guided Imagery To Visualize New Life Situations

(Speak aloud slowly to an individual or group or on to a cassette tape.)

Lie on your back with your palms facing upwards or sit in a comfortable position. Mentally scan your body locating any areas of tension. Direct your attention to those areas and ask your mind to ask your body to let go. Breathe in and out easily and completely, breathing in peace and relaxation and breathing out tension and anxiety. There is something that you want very much. Allow that something to surface in your mind. Look at it. You have wanted this very much. It is a strong desire. Look at it. Feel it. Experience having it with you, near you, touching you. Imagine yourself behaving as if your desire has already been fulfilled. Mentally allow yourself to be in the complete reality of your fulfilled desire. Experience it as if it were happening. Taste it, smell it, feel it, enjoy and experience it. Do this now. Imagine yourself participating in life as though your desire were a reality. Imagine what clothes you would be wearing, what you would be doing, what you might be saying. Fully engage and participate in this mental image. Fully allow yourself to feel what you might feel were this desire an accepted part of your life. Allow the feeling to wash over you. Now allow that mental image, along with the desire, to rise out of your mind. Imagine it slowly floating from your mental screen into the air, until you can barely see it anymore, and let it go. With a content, fulfilled feeling simply turn it over to a higher source. Let it go and enjoy the process. You have fulfilled your desire in your mind and now you can let it go. Good. Slowly and whenever you feel ready allow your consciousness to return to the room. Whenever you feel ready you may open your eyes.

E X E R C I S E

84

Letting Go
Of Tension

A Guided Imagery For Releasing Anxiety And Tension

(Speak aloud slowly to an individual or group or on to a cassette tape.)

Lie on your back or sit comfortably in a chair. Uncross your legs and arms and allow your body to relax naturally. Move your body around and make sounds to let go of any surface tension you may be carrying around. Give the full weight of your body to the floor you are lying on or the chair you are sitting on and ask your mind to ask your body to relax. Allow yourself to be surrounded by a healing light. Breathe that light into your body, letting it fill with luminescence. Breathe out any tension or anxiety. Inhale peace and exhale all negativity. Focus on a circle in the center of your chest and breathe light into that area. Exhale exhaustion and disappointment. Breathe in ease and lightness and exhale dread and suspicion. Breathe in and out easily and completely without a pause between inhalation and exhalation. Visualize an orange liquid in your body. Allow that liquid to absorb like a sponge any remaining stress or anxiety that you may be holding on to. Now release the liquid out of your body, directing it to flow out from your fingertips and the tips of your toes onto the floor. Allow the opaque liquid to carry all tension and fear from your being and in its place allow yourself to be filled up with ease and light and relaxation. I am a beautiful person just the way I am. I am good inside. I like myself and others like me. I feel good about myself. Breathe in and out easily and completely without a pause between inhalation and exhalation, breathing in peace and harmony and out disharmony. Slowly, when I feel ready, I will allow my consciousness to return to this room. I will begin to move my hands and feet and whenever I feel I want to I will open my eyes and be present in the room.

85

Releasing Negativity

A Guided Imagery To Let Go Of Negative Thoughts

(Speak aloud slowly to an individual or group or on to a cassette tape.)

Close your eyes and begin to relax. Allow all tension and anxiety to leave your body. Move around if you need to, make noise to release tension. Go ahead and ask your mind to ask your body to relax. Breathe in and out easily and completely, letting go of the concerns of the day. Allow them to pass through your mind as you quietly observe and remain uninvolved. Feel as if you are sitting on the bank of a river watching the river go by, with no thought of controlling the river as it passes. I have a body but I am not the body. I have a mind but I am not the mind. Breathe in and out easily and completely without a pause between inhalation and exhalation. I am something infinite and I am where I am supposed to be. I am light and love and I love my Self. I will allow any negativity that I may have been carrying around with me to rise to the surface of my consciousness. Slowly my negative thoughts are forming a cloud in the surface of my mind. I watch as they gather together. I see them collect in all of their intensity and strength. I will surround my negative thoughts and images with light and I will allow them to lift. I simply observe as they float away, with no thought of controlling them in any way. I observe as they float farther and farther away from my being. They are going up, up —

higher and higher — they are disappearing. I know that I am where I am meant to be at this point in time. I have a right to be there. I am the creator of my state of mind. Slowly, when I am ready, I will allow my consciousness to return to this room. Whenever I feel ready I will begin to move my body and when I feel like it I will open my eyes and be present in the room.

EXERCISE 86

I Believe In Myself

A Guided Imagery To Enhance Self-Esteem

(Speak aloud slowly to an individual or group or on to a cassette tape.)

Lie or sit comfortably, allowing your body to relax and let go of tension. Move about if you need to, get into a comfortable position and simply let go of any negativity or tension you may have brought with you. As your day runs through your mind or thoughts arise that create anxiety, let them pass before your inner mind with no attempt to involve yourself with them or to chase after them. You do so many things in your day to maintain your work or your family. Take some time now just for yourself, time to turn your focus inward and to be with yourself. Time to find a quiet space within yourself to just be. Breathe in and out easily and completely and let whatever tension may be left drain out of your body and down through the floor.

Ask your mind to ask your body to relax. Let your mind travel through your body searching out any tightness, going to the central point of that tightness and releasing it. Release and exhale any un-wanted feelings, or sensations. Inhale quiet and relaxation, exhale negativity and stress, inhale peace and serenity. Breathe in and out easily and completely and allow the feeling of relaxation to deepen.

Today I take stock of where I am and find that I am okay. I will take care of myself and believe in myself. Today I cast my vote for me, I endorse myself as a candidate for life. I am a good person and I have a right to be here. I believe in myself. I feel that good things will happen for me and I am ready to let myself accept my greater good. I believe in myself. I surround myself with light, vibrating energy, protective energy, life-giving energy. I am a wave of bliss on an ocean of bliss. I feel good inside. Slowly I begin to move my body and let my mind float back into this room. In a few moments, whenever I feel ready, I will come back to this room and be present in it.

87

Three Wishes

A Guided Imagery To Teach People To Wish And Dream

(Speak aloud slowly to an individual or group or on to a cassette tape.)

Lie on your back with your palms facing upwards or sit in a comfortable position. Let your breath flow in and out, filling you with a sense of ease and softness and light. Allow any tension you may be storing to leave you on the out-breath and relax. Breathe in and out easily and completely without a pause between inhalation and exhalation. Mentally move through your body locating any areas of tension and directing those muscles to let go. Breathe in and out easily and completely without a pause between the inhalation and the exhalation and relax. Allow your mind to drift to a peaceful place. Let any distracting thoughts simply disappear on the horizon of your mind and allow yourself to go deeper and deeper. There is something that you have been wanting. Allow that wish to surface now. Look at it. Enjoy it. Imagine how it would feel if it came true. Allow yourself to feel a complete part of it. Then, whenever you feel ready, let it go. You have been granted three wishes. You have two more. Take some time and wish them in any way that you choose. Feel a part of them and enjoy them fully. Take a few minutes and do that now. (Allow a couple of minutes for people to do this process — it may be useful to play some soft music.) Wish them, enjoy them, and let them go. Let them drift off slowly and watch them as they go. Take another minute or two to complete this process. These are your wishes coming from deep inside of you. Everybody has a right to wish. Slowly and whenever you feel ready, bring your consciousness back into the room. Begin to move your fingers and toes and whenever you feel ready, open your eyes.

Variations:

Growing up in homes where there is dysfunction, we lose the ability to wish in a healthy way. We either feel that nothing we wish for could come true and so we never wish at all, assuming that we have no ability to change our lives, or we lose ourselves in a fantasy world split off from reality and our real feelings, where wishing also does not happen because we are disassociated from our feelings from which we wish. A latency age child (6 to 12 years old) will correct traumatic experience through imagination. They will enter into a world of fantasy and symbolization or in sleep they will dream and wake up in the morning as if the traumatic event had never taken place, feeling renewed and refreshed.

Once the ability for abstract thought is developed we lose some access to that corrective world of fantasy. Along with our increased ability to understand reality comes an increased ability to be disheartened and wounded by a reality that is overly inconsistent or dysfunctional. In our sadness we either gave up dreaming or had dreams that were so out of reach that we never had to be responsible for them. They were, after all, unattainable. In recovery we need to learn to wish again, to choose to have dreams for ourselves that are realistic. A healthy life includes healthy dreams and wishes.

88

Letting Go Of Judgment

A Guided Imagery For Cleaning Out Old Judgmental Inner Hopes

(Speak aloud slowly to an individual or group or on to a cassette tape.)

Lie on your back with your palms facing upwards or sit in a comfortable position. Let your breath flow in and out, filling you with a sense of ease and softness and light. Allow any tension you may be storing to leave you on the out-breath and relax. Breathe in and out easily and completely without a pause between inhalation and exhalation. Mentally move through your body locating any areas of tension and directing those muscles to let go. Breathe in and out easily and completely without a pause between the inhalation and the exhalation and relax. Allow your mind to drift to a peaceful place. Let any distracting thoughts simply disappear on the horizon of your mind and allow yourself to go deeper and deeper. Imagine yourself doing something you feel awkward doing or that you feel you do badly. See yourself as you struggle through this activity. Watch yourself and feel the embarrassment that you experience at these times. Tune in your hearing until you can hear the voices of judgment that are running through your mind. Slow down your awareness so that you can hear the exact words that the voices are saying. They may be the same words over and over again or they may be several voices. Listen for one message that is stronger than all the rest. What is it saying? Who is saying it? Place those words in a large container and remove them from the place where they are in your mind. What would you like to do with those words? Do it now, in any way that feels comfortable take an inner action towards those words. Good. Now, whatever form the words are in, wrap them up and let them rise up, up and away from your consciousness. Let them go and forgive yourself for having taken them into your heart. They need no longer have power over you. Understand that the person who said them is not you and need not control you in any way. Let them go. Forgive it all. I am my own best friend. I will treat myself with kindness. I will protect my heart. Slowly and whenever you feel ready, bring your consciousness back into the room and when you wish to, open your eyes.

E X E R C I S E  89

I Am A
Block Of Ice

A Guided Imagery To Encourage Sensory Awareness

(Speak aloud slowly to an individual or group or onto a cassette tape.)

Find a comfortable space on the floor and lie down. Lie on your back and let your arms fall comfortably to your sides. Move around until you feel that you have gotten all the twitches out and you can settle in quietly on the floor.

Breathe in and out three times — breathe in through your nose and out through your mouth. When you breathe in feel that you are breathing in quiet and relaxation and when you breathe out let all the tension and funny feelings leave your mind and your body. Breathe in and out easily and completely.

Let's imagine that your body is made of ice. Feel freezing coldness all over your body — in your head, arms, hands, shoulders, your tummy is very cold, your legs and feet and toes are cold. Your whole body is very tense and cold.

Now imagine that a warm sun is high above your head. It is coming to warm you up. It feels so good on your cold body. It was cold and now it's getting warmer. Everything begins to feel warm and very pleasant.

Slowly, the sun is melting your frozen body. Your head begins to melt. The water is dripping down from your head into the ground beneath you. Your neck and shoulders are getting warmer and melting.

177

Your arms and your hands are going from very cold to very warm and they are melting into the ground. Your chest and waist and hips are slowly melting into the ground. The sun is shining down on your legs and they begin to melt. Slowly your feet melt into the ground beneath you. Feel as if your body is disappearing into the ground. Now breathe in and out easily and completely. When you breathe in, let a feeling of light come over you. When you breathe out, let any feelings you don't like leave your body. Now slowly and whenever you feel ready, open your eyes and move your body.

EXERCISE *90*

I Am A Rainbow

A Guided Imagery To Encourage Creative Writing

(Speak aloud slowly to an individual or group or onto a cassette tape.)

Today it is a beautiful day. I will lie down on my back and be very still. I will let my body just relax right into the floor.

Today is a beautiful day and just for a moment I will put all my cares and worries into a grey cloud that is passing overhead and let them float away.

Just for now I will close my eyes and imagine that the sky is a deep blue, that the sun is shining softly making me feel warm and safe and that there is a very soft breeze passing over me making me feel light and happy.

Today I know that I am beautiful like the sky, warm like the sun and soft like the breeze.

I breathe in and I think of filling my body with yellow light from the top of my head to the tips of my toes. I breathe in and out and I let all my feelings that I don't like go out of my body. I breathe in yellow light and I breathe out unwanted feelings. I breathe in peacefulness and I breathe out restlessness.

I am like a feather floating on the soft wind. I am like a ray of sunlight shining on the earth. I let my body relax. I let my shoulders and arms relax. I let my hips and legs relax. I let my feet and toes relax.

I am like a rainbow created by different colors inside me. When I walk I feel wonderful and powerful. I am a good person with my own special way of being and understanding. It feels good to be here and I belong here.

Slowly, I come back to my body lying on the floor. Slowly, I feel my head, my arms, my legs. I breathe in and out in an easy, pleasant way.

Today I feel like a rainbow and I will share my colors with myself and others around me.

Slowly, I let my eyes open and begin to move. Today when I open my eyes I think I will see rainbows everywhere.

E X E R C I S E

91

Releasing Numbness

A Guided Imagery To Return Feeling And Inner Awareness

(Speak aloud slowly to an individual or group or onto a cassette tape.)

Lie comfortably on your back with your palms facing the ceiling or sit up straight with your head, neck and trunk in an elongated position. Breathe in and out easily and completely without a pause between inhalation and exhalation and ask your mind to ask your body to relax. Beginning at the bottom of your body, imagine breathing in new life and fresh energy and breathing out old, tired energy and stuckness. Relax your feet, relax your toes, your heels, the balls of your feet, the tops of your feet, and allow them to fill with a new energy as you breathe tiredness out and lightness in. Relax your calves, relax your knees, relax your thighs; breathe in and out easily and completely without a pause between inhalation and exhalation. Relax your hips and let your breath carry out any tension or anxiety that may be stored in that area as you breathe in a new tingling sensation and light, happy energy. Relax your abdomen; let your breath fill it like a colorful balloon, then press it out as the balloon releases the air light and easy and very relaxed. Relax your chest. Let it fill with white light until the light emanates from your chest within and without, each breath is beautiful and full of cleansing light. Relax your shoulders. Let the muscles in your shoulders let go now. Imagine that a feeling

181

of warmth is slowly expanding, going deep into the muscle, making it feel soft and elastic. Breathe in and out easily and completely, breathing in vibrating energy, scanning your body to locate any numb areas, then breathing out that area of numbness — breathe it out and let it leave your body completely. Fill the area instead with soft, vibrating white light.

I am a vibrant being. I give and receive energy. I am in harmony with the life within me and without me. I am supple and flexible. I respond to life fully and spontaneously. I can accept being open to myself and open to my surroundings. I let go of the pockets of deadness and numbness that I allowed to be stored in my body. I give them back now. I allow them to rise from me and dissipate in the atmosphere. I am fully alive and willing to experience life. I love myself and I respect my rights to feel full and free. I have the capacity to feel all my feelings. I have the ability to enjoy life.

Slowly I feel a soft vibrating light passing through my body beginning at my feet and moving upward through my legs, slowly up now, passing through my hips, torso, arms and chest, creating a tingling sensation, deliciously alive, into my shoulders, a soft vibrating light on my skin, within my neck and head. My whole body feels receptive and in tune. I am beautiful as I am. I love myself as I am. I can take care of myself and I will be good to myself.

Slowly, bring your consciousness back to the room and whenever you feel ready, open your eyes.

A
C

EXERCISE *92*

Unfinished Business

A Guided Imagery To Complete Unfinished Business On A Mental And Emotional Level

(Speak aloud slowly to an individual or group or onto a cassette tape.)

Lie down in a comfortable position with your palms facing the ceiling and your feet gently falling to the sides, or sit up straight with your head, neck and trunk in an elongated position. Focus your attention on your breath and ask your mind to ask your body to relax. Mentally move around your body. Locate any areas where you are holding your muscles tightly or storing tension. Breathe in relaxation and let go of the tension in each area with a deep exhalation. Allow every part of your body to feel light and relaxed. Breathe in and out easily and completely without a pause between inhalation and exhalation and relax. In your mind slowly visualize a door. What color is the door? What is its size? What is it made of? What does the handle look like? Slowly approach the door. Now turn the handle and enter the room inside. What does the room look like? What color are the walls? How high is the ceiling? Does it have windows? What furniture is in the room? What is the light like in the room? Now you notice that someone is in the room with you. Are they standing or sitting? What is their body position? What is the expression on their face? How do you feel when you see them? Do you engage them in any way? If you find yourself

183

speaking to them what are you saying? What is the tone of your voice? Go ahead and say what you want to say. This moment is all yours to say what you need to say. Say everything. Say all of it. Speak your truth clearly. (Pause and allow another minute or two of silence while they finish.) Now say the last thing you would like to say to this person. Good. You have said what you needed to say. Release any lingering feelings that surround this and relax. Return to your breathing and breathe in and out easily and completely without a pause between inhalation and exhalation. Slowly bring your awareness back into the room. Begin to wiggle your toes and feet. Whenever you feel ready, you may open your eyes.

Variation:

After doing this exercise, participants may wish to share their visualizations with the group or to use the letter writing or journal exercises.

93

Moving Through Emotional Blocks

A Guided Imagery To Move Inwardly Through Blocks

(Speak aloud slowly to an individual or group or onto a cassette tape.)

Lie on your back in a comfortable position with your palms facing up and your feet gently falling to the sides, or sit up straight with your head, neck and trunk in an elongated position. Breathe in and out easily and completely, breathing out any tension or anxiety that may be stored in your body. Ask your mind to ask your body to relax. Allow your thoughts to move through your consciousness while you simply watch without any attempt to enter into them or control them. Simply be a passive observer and continue to allow your relaxation to deepen. Breathe in and out easily and completely, breathing in light or ease and breathing out tension and tightness. And relax. Imagine that you have a screen in your mind. Allow to appear on the screen something you find difficult to do; anything you have a block about that you feel holds you back from living your life fully and happily. Place that scene on your mental screen and simply observe it. Simply observe with no thought of entering into the scene or controlling it. Note the feelings that arise. Allow them to come over you and leave you without attempting to control them or work with them in any way. Now we are going to visually move back from the scene and into a comfortable place. Locate a safe space where you feel completely at ease. Allow yourself to be there in your mind's eye and on your mental screen. Enjoy the safety. Absorb the comfort. Slowly, as you feel ready, prepare to do that thing that you are uncomfortable doing. Put down anything you may be holding, pick up anything that you may need to have with you and begin to move toward that situation. If anywhere in this process anxiety arises, simply pause for a moment and return to your relaxation breathing — breathe deeply and fully, allowing a sense of ease and inner control to fill you up on the inhalation and release any anxiety or fear on the exhalation. Then return to your activity, pausing whenever you need to regain a sense of serenity and inner control, then return once again to your activity and proceed to move through it. Repeat this process until you have imagined yourself doing that thing that you are uncomfortable doing in its entirety, until you have moved through it completely. Do this visualization on your own until you are completely comfortable in this activity, each time pausing and returning to your breath when you need to and thanking yourself and congratulating yourself when you move through it. Slowly, whenever you feel ready, bring your consciousness back into the room and gently open your eyes.

Variations:

Each group member may wish to share their experience of this exercise, both the situation that they have trouble with and the feelings they feel around it. You may also work through the situation psychodramatically with role play if you choose.

E X E R C I S E 94

Inner Guide

A Guided Imagery To Get In Touch With Your Inner Wisdom

(Speak aloud slowly to an individual or group or onto a cassette tape.)

Lie on the floor in a comfortable position with your palms facing up and your feet falling gently to the sides, or sit up straight with your head, neck and trunk in an elongated position. Allow your breathing to become smooth and even and let your mind and your body relax. Mentally scan your body. If you notice any tense places in your body release them now, allowing the tension to leave and float away. I am going to count from 10 to one. As I do this visualize each number in your mind, and as you release each number release tension along with it. 10-9-8-7-6-5-4-3-2-1. (Say these numbers very slowly. In between some of the numbers you may say "breathe in and out easily and completely" or "letting go of more tension.") In the distance you see a mountain. Slowly you approach it and begin to climb. Farther and farther up you make your way. Imagine yourself climbing the last few feet to a plateau. It has a beautiful clearing and peacefully, in the middle of it, sits a person in quiet contemplation. Slowly approach this person and sit down near them. Allow a question to arise in your mind and then ask it. Wait patiently while the answer comes. Allow yourself to absorb the answer and to feel gratitude toward your own inner guides for their perceptive understanding. This is a spiritual place within you that you may come to whenever you feel the need. This guide lives always within you. Express your respect and gratitude to this guide within you. Slowly allow yourself to move and let your breathing bring you back into the room. Whenever you feel ready you may open your eyes.

Variations:

You may reverse roles with your inner guide a few times if it seems useful.

EXERCISE 95

Body Voices

A Guided Imagery To Explore Somatized Feelings

(Speak aloud slowly to an individual or group or onto a cassette tape.)

Lie on your back with your palms facing the ceiling or sit in a comfortable position. Mentally scan your body for any tense areas. Breathe into those areas and allow the muscles to release the tension they're holding. Breathe in and out easily and completely without a pause between inhalation and exhalation and ask your mind to ask your body to relax.

Observe the thoughts that are passing through your mind. Let them pass before you on the screen of your mind while you simply watch, making no attempt to enter into them or in any way control them. Notice how one thought leads to another thought, one image gives way to another image. Now allow yourself to experience the feelings that are connected to your thoughts. Allow the feelings to surface and let yourself feel them as they arise. Notice if the feeling seems to be located in any particular part of your body then continue to let it arise as you experience it. Pay attention to the feeling it creates in your body — notice how your body feels when you feel this feeling. Where is the feeling? How far does it extend? Does it travel? If this feeling had a voice what would the voice sound like? Would it be high or low, shrill or soft, strong or weak? Allow yourself to imagine the words that this voice might say. Do this for another minute. Slowly let the voice fade away and get fainter. Let it disappear. Whenever you feel ready, begin to move your fingers and toes and gradually bring your attention back into the room.

Variations:

You may change your position and reverse roles with the voice if it seems appropriate. Refer to "I am a feeling" for next exercise.

EXERCISE 96

A Visit With My Inner Child

A Guided Imagery To Get In Touch With The Inner Child

(Speak aloud slowly to an individual or group or onto a cassette tape.)

Today we are going within to visit with our inner child. Whenever we take time with our inner child we give ourselves the opportunity to heal a little more. In the same way that our bodies are nourished with food, our hearts and spirits are nourished by the life of our own child within. This is a gift that we can give ourselves, the gift of time — just to be. I am going to allow myself the time and space to visit with the child who lives within me because that is a good and safe place to be.

Lie comfortably on your back, let your arms fall to your sides with your palms facing up and allow your feet to fall easily to the sides. Breathe in and out easily and completely without a pause between inhalation and exhalation and ask your mind to ask your body to relax. Relax your forehead. Relax your eyes, relax your cheeks, relax your ears, relax your mouth and tongue, relax your jaw, relax your neck, relax your shoulders, relax your arms, relax your hands, relax your fingers and fingertips. Breathe in and out easily and completely. Let the weight of your body sink into the floor, breathing out any tension that still may be in your body and breathing in peace and relaxation. Relax your chest, relax your abdomen, relax your pelvis, relax your legs, relax your feet and the soles of your feet. Breathe in and out easily and completely and then let the relaxation deepen. I am a wave of bliss on an ocean of bliss. I am in a safe space within myself. I have beauty and light within me that is me. I have an inner child within me that is me and I am going to let that child live and be happy. I am going to honor that child and take good care of it. I will go easy on my inner child and be kind and understanding of its needs. When I open my eyes I will let my child shine through. I will leave room for magic in my day. Slowly I begin to move my hands and feet, letting my consciousness return to the room. Whenever I feel ready I will open my eyes and be present in the room.

Draw a picture of your childhood room and place your child in it.

Write a letter to your child from your adult self telling it how you feel about it.

Draw three faces of your inner child (from long ago or present time) with a sentence underneath each about why they feel the way they do.

Write a description or draw a picture of an event that happened with your family of origin that made you feel good.

Write a description or draw a picture of an event that happened with your family of origin that made you feel bad.

Write a description or draw a picture of something that you wish you had done with your family of origin.

Conclusion

The use of drama as a therapeutic tool dates back to before the birth of Christ. It is the earliest form of therapy that we know of. According to Aristotle . . . *violence is purged by its poetic representation on a stage* . . . The process of purgation is called catharsis from the Greek *Katharsis.* Through re-experiencing a traumatic event within the safe structure of a Greek tragedy or a psychodrama we purge pain that has been stored within the psyche. The poetic representation of psychodramatic dramatization acts as the trigger that allows a person to put their finger on their own pain. Aeschylus knew that there are a few themes that are common to us all, that in our depths we are profoundly alike and he developed plays that addressed the issues most basic to man. In a large psychodrama the same universal themes emerge naturally within the dramatic structure. As Ralph Waldo Emerson said, *To know that what is true for us in the privacy of our own hearts is true for all men, this is genius* . . . That understanding is also at the center of comprehending ourselves and our own spirituality.

The Greek word for sin is *amartea,* which means "to miss the mark." Sin to the ancients was not born of its own source but rather a result of not being in line with the truth within ourselves. It is a reflection of distance from our own souls or God selves. It also implies that it is not only what we learn not to do but what we learn to do that brings us closer to our higher good. The word in Greek for miracle is *thavma,* which means awesome. An occurrence not separate from reality but a part of it. Something beyond expectation, something we thought might never happen but does happen every day.

Healing can hurt. To return to those old situations and the loneliness, sadness and confusion associated with them is painful physically, emotionally and spiritually but then healing happens on its own and when it does it is a quiet miracle, something awesome, and we are, each time, a step closer to the mark.

Resource List

The following is a list of places where more information may be obtained about psychodrama and its use in treatment.

Co-dependency And Experiential Therapy

Anon Anew at Boca Raton, Inc. (800) 368-6222
Boca Raton, FL

Caron Foundation (215) 678-2332
Wernersville, PA.

The Center for Problem Resolution (813) 585-9986
Largo, FL.

Children are People (CAP) (612) 227-4031
St. Paul, MN.

Halterman Center (614) 852-1372
London, OH.

Innerlook, Inc. (212) 787-7914
New York, NY.

The Meadows (602) 271-9160
Phoenix, AZ.

Onsite (605) 341-7432
Rapid City, SD.

Sierra Tucson (602) 624-4000
Tucson, AZ.

Psychodrama Therapy And Training

Institute for Sociotherapy, Inc. (212) 725-0033
New York, NY.

Zerka Moreno (914) 831-2318
Beacon, NY.

American Society for Group Psychotherapy and Psychodrama (ASGPP)
(703) 556-9222

Bibliography

Abraham, Karl. **Clinical Papers and Essays on Psychoanalysis**. New York: Brunner/Mazel, Inc., 1955.

Ackerman, Robert J. **Let Go And Grow: Recovery For Adult Children**. Deerfield Beach, FL: Health Communications, 1987.

Axline, M. Virginia. **Play Therapy**. New York: Ballentine Books, 1947.

Black, Claudia. **It Will Never Happen To Me**. Denver, CO: M.A.E., 1981.

Blatner, Adam. **Acting-In. Practical Applications of Psychodramatic Methods**. New York: Springer Pub., 1983.

Blatner, Adam and Blatner, Alee. **Foundations of Psychodrama: History, Theory & Practice**. New York: Springer Pub., 1988.

Briggs, Dorothy Corkille. **Your Child's Self-Esteem**. New York: Doubleday, 1975.

Elam, Kier. **Semiotics of Theater & Drama**. New York: Routledge Chapman & Hall, 1980.

Elkind, David. **The Hurried Child**. Reading, MA: Addison-Wesley, 1981.

Fox, Jonathan. ed. **The Essential Moreno: Writings on Psychodrama, Group Method & Spontaneity**. New York: Springer Pub., 1987.

Freud, Anna. **Psychoanalysis for Teachers and Parents**. New York: Norton, 1963.

Freud, Sigmund. **On Dreams**. New York: Norton, 1957.

――――――― **A General Selection from the Works of Sigmund Freud**. New York: Doubleday, 1957.

――――――― **Introductory Lectures on Psychoanalysis**. New York: Norton, 1966.

Greenspan, Stanley I and Pollock, George H. **The Course of Life**. Washington: U.S. Dept. of Health and Human Services, 1980.

Hainstock, G. Elizabeth. **The Essential Montessori**. New York: Signet, 1978.

Hartnoll, Phy̠.ᵗ The Theatre: A Concise History. New York: Thames Hudson, 1985.

Hendricks, C. Gaylord and Roberts, Thomas B. The Centering Book. New Jersey: Prentice-Hall.

_____ The Second Centering Book. New Jersey: Prentice-Hall, 1977.

Hendricks, C. Gaylord and Hendricks, Kathryn. The Moving Center. New Jersey: Prentice-Hall, 1983.

Isaacs, Nathan. A Brief Introduction to Piaget. New York: Schocken, 1972.

Jung, C. J. Four Archetypes. New Jersey: Princeton University Press, 1969.

_____ Dreams. New Jersey: Princeton University Press, 1973.

Kritsberg, Wayne. Chronic Shock. Deerfield Beach, FL: Health Communications, 1985.

Lillard, Paula Polk. Montessori, A Modern Approach. New York: Schocken, 1973.

List, Lynne K. Music, Art and Drama Experiences for the Elementary Curriculum. New York: Teachers College Press, 1982.

McCaslin, Nellie. Creative Drama in the Classroom. New York: Longman, 1984.

Mariechild, Diane. Mother Wit: A Feminist Guide to Psychic Development. Freedom, CA: Crossing Press, 1981.

Maslow, Abraham. Toward a Psychology of Being. New York: Van Nos Reinhold, 1968.

Montessori, Maria. The Montessori Method. New York: Schocken, 1964.

_____ Spontaneous Activity in Education. New York: Schocken, 1965.

_____ Dr. Montessori's Own Handbook. New York: Schocken, 1965.

_____ From Childhood to Adolescence. New York: Schocken, 1976.

_____ Education for Human Development. New York: Schocken, 1977.

Moreno, J. L. Group Psychotherapy. New York: Beacon House, 1945.

_____ Sociometry, Experimental Method and the Science of Society. New York: Beacon House, 1951.

O'Gorman, Patricia and Oliver-Diaz, Philip. Breaking The Cycle Of Addiction: For Adult Children Of Alcoholics. Deerfield Beach, FL: Health Communications, 1987.

Penrod, James. Movement for the Performing Artist. Mountain View, CA: Mayfield Pub., 1974.

Piaget, Jean. **Origins of Intelligence in Children**. Madison, CT: Intl Universities Press, 1966.

Rebelsky, Fred and Dorman, Lynn. **Child Development and Behavior**. New York: Knopf, 1970.

Rogers, Carl R. **On Becoming a Person**. Boston, MA: Houghton Mifflin, 1961.

Rohnke, Karl. **Silver Bullets**. Hamilton, ME: Project Adventure, Inc., 1986.

Sarnoff, Charles. **Latency**. New York: Aronson, 1976.

Satir, Virginia. **The New Peoplemaking**. Palo Alto: Science and Behavior Books, Inc., 1988.

Scwebel, Milton and Ralph, Jane. **Piaget in the Classroom**. New York: Basic Books, 1973.

Stanislavski, Constantin. **Creating a Role**. New York: Theatre Arts, 1961.

Subby, Robert. **Lost In The Shuffle: The Co-dependent Reality**. Deerfield Beach, FL: Health Communications, 1987.

Turner, Victor. **From Ritual to Theatre: The Human Seriousness of Play**. New York: PAJ Pub., 1982.

Wegscheider-Cruse, Sharon. **Choicemaking: For Co-dependents, Adult Children And Spirituality Seekers**. Pompano Beach, FL: Health Communications, 1985.

_____ **Learning To Love Yourself: Finding Your Self-Worth**. Deerfield Beach, FL: Health Communications, 1987.

Weinrib, Estelle. **Images of the Self: The Sandplay Therapy Process**. Boston, MA: Sigo Press, 1983.

Winnicott, D.W. **The Child and the Outside World**. London, U.K.: Pelican Books, 1981.

Woititz, Janet G. **Adult Children of Alcoholics**. Pompano Beach, FL: Health Communications, 1983.

Wright, Derek. **The Psychology of Moral Behavior**. New York: Penguin Books, 1981.